RELIGION IN YORKSHIRE
1700 – 2000

SHEILA McGEOWN

BLACKTHORN PRESS

Blackthorn Press, Blackthorn House
Middleton Rd, Pickering YO18 8AL
United Kingdom

www.blackthornpress.com

ISBN 978 1 906259 34 1

© Sheila McGeown 2014

Printed and bound by CPI Group (UK) Ltd, Croydon, CR0 4YY

This book is dedicated to
John Rushton M.B.E.
In love and gratitude

CONTENTS

ACKNOWLEDGEMENTS

I would like to thank all the people who shared their memories with me, for inclusion in this book. Emma Rushton and Christopher Wilson for help with some of the photography, and above all Richard Crocker, without whose generous efforts on my behalf, especially his IT skills, I would not have produced the finished text.

INTRODUCTION

When Pope wrote in 1733 'Know then thyself, presume not God to scan; the proper study of mankind is man' he was the poetic voice of that movement which began to seek answers to problems, not in long held beliefs or dogma from the pulpit but through reasoned argument and verifiable experiment. Illness no longer became God's punishment for wickedness and beyond our understanding but something to be studied and cured. Galileo showed through his observations that the sun was the centre of the solar system, not the earth, although the Catholic Church threatened him so that he was obliged to deny this truth. The scientific method of theory, backed by experiment, tested by one's peers and only then generally accepted as the truth has become the basis of the modern world and is at odds with a system which requires faith but not proof.

The publication of Charles Darwin's 'On the Origin of the Species' in 1859 can be seen as a major blow to fundamental faith. Darwin made clear that the animals and plants and humans themselves were not made in six days by God but had evolved over millions of years. If the story of Genesis was just a story, what other parts of the bible were not literally true? Gradually, it became accepted by all but the most fundamental of Christians that the bible was a mixture of history, folk tales and legend. The life of Christ was examined by German scholars such as Strauss and the conclusion was that the man Jesus did probably exist yet the version of his life told in the New Testament was again a mixture of history and allegory, much influenced by the needs of the early church.

The carnage of the first world war shook many men's beliefs. Those who did come back home safely found it hard to reconcile the notion of a loving God with the horrors they had lived through. This general feeling was reflected in the poetry of Sassoon, Owen and many others.

These ideas were not broadly known or accepted by the general public but gradually they filtered down. Some clergymen like the Bishop of Woolwich attempted to address the general public and wrote 'Honest to God' in 1963, a popular theology which tried to reconcile the new ideas to old beliefs. They probably did little to attract new members but confirmed many doubters in their rejection of formal religion.

The arts had an important place to play in this reduction in the respect paid to organised religion. Priests had had their critics from the days of Chaucer, writing in the 14th Century, 'A Friar there was / a wanton and a merry' and Trollope in the 19th century was not afraid in his Barchester novels to show the clergy with all their foibles and even made them the villains, 'He did not believe in the Gospel with more assurance than he did in the sacred justice of all ecclesiastical revenues.' But the real onslaught came in the twentieth century when clergymen began to appear on the stage as figures of fun in countless farces and the theme was taken up by television with vicars and priests becoming increasingly laughed at, however kindly, in programmes such as 'The Vicar of Dibley', 'Father Ted' and 'Dad's Army'. Eventually, priests became sinister figures to be feared in the novels of Dan Brown.

The scandals which rocked the Catholic Church as case after case, around the world, began to unfold of sexual abuse of children by priests and the attempt by the church to cover up this and other crimes, shook the belief of many and made it almost impossible for the Church to recruit new priests in this country. Taken in conjunction with the evidence that in Ruanda, Catholic priests were among those who incited the genocide and that the Catholic dogma against the use of contraceptives has been a major cause in the spread of the aids epidemic, the churches hostility to homosexuals and the refusal to allow priests to marry or women to become priests means that the Catholic religion is becoming more the religion of the poor and uneducated. Italy, the heart of Catholicism, has one of the lowest birth rates in Europe and attendance at mass, especially amongst the young, is falling.

And yet, in the last census of 2011 when people in the United Kingdom were asked to state their religion, 60% claimed to be Christian. But only 6% attended a place of worship on a regular basis. Since the abolition of Sunday closing in 1994, there were many other more attractive things to do on a Sunday. Churches, with their expensive buildings and staff, their antiquated costumes and language and the endless sexual scandals, their refusal to allow women at first as clergy and then as bishops, seem increasingly out of touch with multi-cultural, liberal Britain. Those churches which do thrive seem to the outsider to be fundamental, hysterical and somehow not British. The young are turning increasingly to non-Christian religions such as paganism or a form of nature worship.

This book looks in detail at religion in Yorkshire over three hundred years. In 1700, Yorkshire, like the rest of England, was dominated architecturally and legally, if not entirely spiritually, by the Church of England. From its great minsters at York, the seat of the Archbishop of York, Ripon, and Beverley down to the humblest of parish churches, every citizen of Yorkshire was allotted a parish and a place to worship in that parish.

Indeed, it was against the law not to attend the Church of England's services or to pay the taxes it demanded for its upkeep in the form or tithes and church rates. Those who refused to pay had their property taken and were often imprisoned. Church and State went hand in hand and were mutually supportive. To this day, the Archbishop of Canterbury places the crown on the head of the monarch and the monarch appoints the Prime Minister. The Church of England is part of 'The Establishment' which governs this country. Yet despite the fact that twenty-six Anglican bishops sit in the House of Lords, the law is now mainly secular. Authors cannot be prosecuted for blasphemy or, since the Lady Chatterley trial, indecency. The law does not allow muslims to mutilate their daughters or Jehova's Witnesses to let their childred die for want of a blood transfusion. It is no longer against the law to be a homosexual or to commit suicide despite a vocal religious lobby. Human rights are more important than religious beliefs.

The religious infrastructure had been inherited from the Roman Catholic Church in the sixteenth century when Henry VIII, driven by his desire for Anne Boleyn and his need for a male heir, set up his own church and broke with Rome. Not that the Catholics went away. Few had the courage of Thomas More or Margaret Clitherow of York, who were ready to die for their faith but many kept up the 'old faith' quietly and surreptitiously, supporting itinerant priests and taking the Mass in secret. Catholics did not always help their cause and they were frequently behind plots to remove the monarch and restore Catholicism, most famously when Guy Fawkes, who was born in York, came close to blowing up King and Parliament in 1605 and as late as 1745 Catholics supported 'Bonny Prince Charley' on his march to London. To be a Catholic was seen as being equivalent to being a traitor, much as being a Muslim today can seen by some as being equivalent to being a terrorist. By 1767 it was estimated that Catholics made up only 1% of the population. Following the removal by 1829 of all legal restraints to being a Catholic and the influx of Irish and Polish workers who were mainly Catholic, the figure had risen to 12% by 2001, although not all of these attend mass. However, it is still against the law for an English monarch to be a Catholic, although from 2008 it became legal for a monarch to marry one, and there has never been a Catholic Prime Minister.

Despite its seeming dominance, all was not as solid as it seemed in the Church of England. By 1850, there were two broad camps among its ranks. There was the 'High Church', the right wing, leaning towards Catholicism and the 'Low Church', the more left wing, heirs to the Protestant revolution who liked things simple and plain. Although Methodism, a powerful force in much of Yorkshire, began life as part of the Anglican community, it soon took on its own life and became a separate church, appealing to the lower social orders, often ignored by the upper class clergy. By the late twentieth century a third force,

'Evangelicalism' much favoured by the African and Caribbean Anglicans, began to attract large congregations. These three forces tugged and pulled at the Anglican Church's unity, often to the despair of the Archbishop of Canterbury who tried to steer a middle path, holding it all together.

And then there were the Jews and the dissenters, those who refused to accept the authority of either the Anglican Church or Catholic Church but went their own way both in forms of worship and belief. From Unitarians to Quakers, each brought variety and practical Christianity to the religious life of Yorkshire. The immigration of workers into Yorkshire from India and Pakistan added the Muslim religion to the mix and towns like Bradford saw the minaret rise alongside the spire.

But despite all these differences, the fundamental beliefs of most Englishmen were the same in 1700 and did not change much down to the present time. God was in heaven and had created this world. His word was transmitted to us through the Bible which was literally true. He had sent his son, Jesus Christ, who was crucified to take on our sins and through him we could be saved and expect a place in heaven.

The theme of this book is how this certainty gave way in the course of three hundred years to one of doubt, indifference and even hostility to religion, when attending a place of worship became the unusual rather than the norm and the role of priest lost much of its kudos and respectability.

The statistics are clearly set out in the following chapters. Despite flourishes of zeal and occasional rising attendances, this was patchy and depended on a charismatic leader or a new way of worshiping, often brought in by American preachers. The overall trend in attendance at places of worship was inexorably down.

What were the reasons for this decline in formal religion? From the Enlightenment and Scientific Revolution of the seventeenth century to the militant atheism of the twentieth, the story is one of increasing doubt and then disbelief as the evidence against the fundamental beliefs of the Christian and other religions accumulated.

Alan Avery 2014

ILLUSTRATIONS

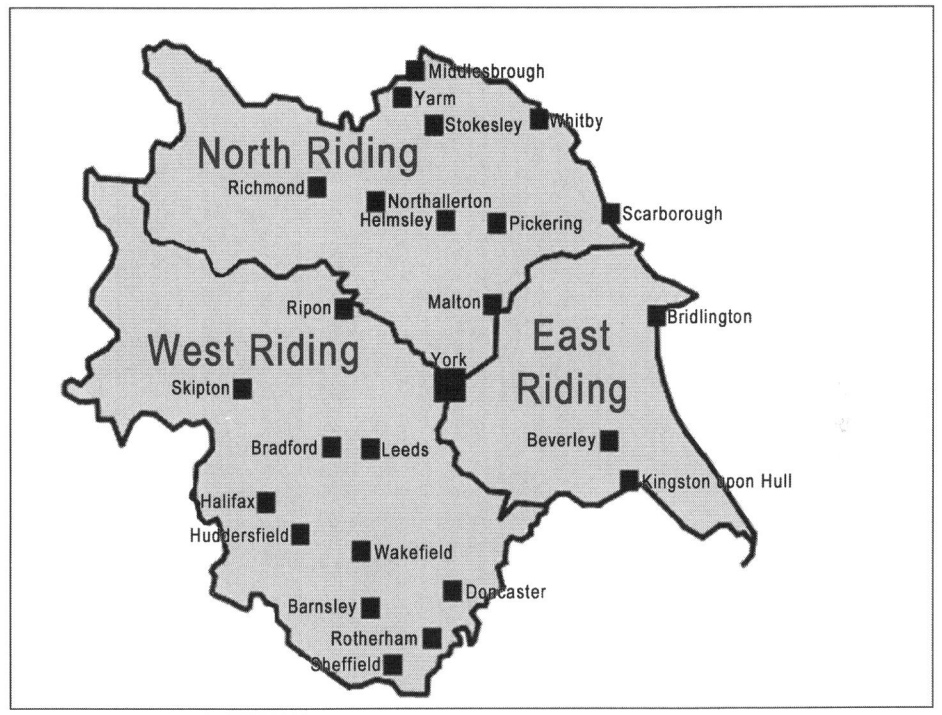

Map 1. Yorkshire's main towns and cities

CHAPTER 1

RELIGION IN YORKSHIRE IN THE EIGHTEENTH CENTURY

From the Reformation in the middle of the 16th century, until the end of the 17th century, religion in England had been controversial. It affected a large number of people, whose beliefs and practices ranged from those of the determined adherents to the Roman Catholic Church, whose allegiance to the Pope made them suspect to a protestant government, through more accommodating and conforming church papists, moderate Anglicans, to less or more extreme protestant dissenting congregations and Quakers.

In 1698, the Toleration Act made life easier for protestant dissenters, but no such toleration was allowed for Catholics. If they were careful in their behaviour they were usually left alone, especially as they were often connected to a gentry family with money and local influence. When national crises arose however, they could still be, and occasionally were, heavily penalised for their beliefs.

In addition to the people with genuine religious beliefs of whatever kind, there was also the unknown number of people who may or may not have attended church, except for baptisms, marriages and certainly burials. If it was politic for some of these people to attend church, they no doubt did so. Others never did, despite such absence being illegal.

Even though there was a strong belief in a Christian God running through the lives of many of the English population at the beginning of the 18th century, there was, especially in the countryside, a strong belief in witchcraft and other superstitions.

There were also differences of theological belief between English Protestants. Many people, especially Presbyterians and Independents, were Calvinists. They believed in predestination. That a person was born to go to heaven as a member of the 'elect', or they were not. If the latter, nothing that person did in their earthly life would make any difference at their death. They would not go to heaven. Other Christians were Arminians, who believed in free will, and that the Grace of God was available to all mankind.

The Anglican Church or Church of England was the established church. It had a hierarchy of Archbishops, Bishops, Archdeacons, Deans, and sundry other officers. At ground roots level was the parish, which had a church with a

1 Saint James Ravenfield West Riding built in 1756 by John Carr. One of a very limited number of Anglican churches built in the eighteenth century

parson. The parson could be a rector, a vicar or a perpetual curate. They had the 'living' which included an appropriate house, and sometimes a farm, (glebe). A rector also received the great tithes of the parish. A vicar or perpetual curate had the lesser tithes. All were entitled to fees for performing baptisms, marriages and funerals, known as surplice fees. The value of a living depended on the size and wealth of the parish.

If these men did not live in their parish, they were supposed to pay a stipendiary curate to act as their deputy, i.e. to perform divine service in the church every Sunday, to administer the sacrament, to prepare children for confirmation and to minister to the sick and needy of their parish.

Where the parish was extensive, there could be one or more chapels of ease, where parishioners could go to Sunday Service. Some of these would have their own curate, who would have baptised, married and buried the inhabitants of the 'chapelry', or they may have had to attend the parish church for such occasions.

In Yorkshire, as in the rest of England, at the beginning of the 18th century there was much in the established church that was wrong. A large number of clergy looked on their profession as an income for life rather than a vocation. Many were younger sons or from cadet branches of the gentry and some of those had little interest in spiritual matters and rarely put themselves to any trouble on behalf of their flock. In order to afford a wealthy lifestyle, they would have more than one parish, where they paid a curate a meagre stipend to minister to the parish on their behalf.

Such curates, if married with families, frequently acted for more than one clergyman in order to make enough to live on, thereby making it almost impossible to give the people of the parish sufficient help and guidance, spiritual or otherwise.

When people attended Sunday service, they frequently endured sermons, of incredible dullness read without spontaneity. They sat, if they were lucky enough to rent or own a pew, otherwise they stood, in cold and draughty churches. The standing poor were made to feel their lack of status, consequently many did not attend. Indeed, had all the parishioners attended at one time, it is unlikely that some churches would have contained them, and this at a time when the population was increasing.

There was an awareness of a need for spiritual improvement of the established church, but many clerics at all levels appear to have been more concerned with maintaining the status quo, and the preservation of good morals and orderly behaviour, rather than the spiritual health of their flocks.

2. Hogarth's cartoon of an 18th century church service

3. Archbishop John Sharp 1644 - 1714

The head of the church in Yorkshire was the Archbishop of York. Throughout the 18th century, the men who held that position were many things; the better ones were politicians, good administrators, courtiers even, but few were spiritual men. The poorer sort were lazy absentees, epicureans and one sexually immoral.

The best was Archbishop John Sharp who did try to reduce the number of parishes held in plurality, though even he was not immune to promoting his friends and family. A puritan, he was a supporter of the religious societies which were founded around the turn of the century to meet a perceived need among young Anglican men for an exchange of spiritual experiences and ideas, and for prayers. He also encouraged the more enduring Anglican Society for the Promotion of Christian Knowledge founded in 1698 with the aim of promoting charity schools, making bibles and religious tracts readily available, and generally advancing the honour of God. He was close to Queen Anne and had some input in establishing Queen Anne's Bounty in 1704, whereby poor livings were financially augmented.

It would be wrong to think that there were not a considerable number of ordinary people to whom a quiet and trusting belief in an Anglican God formed the bedrock of their lives in the 18th century. Such a man was James Fretwell, of Barnby Dun in south Yorkshire, described in his will as a yeoman; and a man, according to his diary not overly preoccupied with religion. He wrote the following on the death of his mother in 1736,

> 'The foundation in us of everything that is good is chiefly owing (under God) to her pious care and maternal instruction, which was seconded by her praying with and for us.'

Wealthier and more influential people made a much larger impact. Lady Elizabeth Hastings inherited the estate of Ledstone in 1705, when she was 24 years old. According to her half-sister Lady Anne, she,

> 'had always a religious frame of mind'.

Long before the Wesleys made their impact, Lady Betty, as she was known, practiced a 'methodical' life of devotion, both personal and with her family and friends. Ralph Thoresby was a guest at Ledstone Hall on January 5th 1723. He recorded in his diary for that day that he,

> 'read till family prayers; then with the three ladies till the vicar of Ledsham came to read the church prayers. After dinner the ladies took the air; upon their return ....the parson read the evening service. After supper, had a religious conference.'

Lady Betty and her sisters and friends were part of the early evangelical movement which was the most important influence on religion in 18th century England. This movement's most lasting achievement was the founding of Methodism, but the established church and some dissenting churches were also heavily involved in its drive for more vital and inclusive Christian belief and behaviour.

During the 1730's the ladies of Ledstone Hall flirted with Methodism. Lady Betty was a patroness of the Holy Club founded by John Wesley at Oxford. Her letters show an interest in the work of George Whitefield.

They attended the services of Benjamin Ingham, one of the major promoters of early evangelicalism in Yorkshire, and were sufficiently impressed by his preaching to invite him to Ledstone Hall. In 1741 he married Lady Margaret Hastings. She in turn was responsible for the conversion of her sister in law Selina, Countess of Huntington, who formed her own branch of Methodism, known as 'The Countess of Huntington's Connexion'. The other two sisters followed, and actively engaged in a preaching tour of Wales in 1748.

Lady Betty remained an Anglican, and put her money and effort into founding charity schools and other charitable institutions. She believed that as the Methodist movement grew it began to depart from the order and discipline of the Anglican Church.

In the middle of the 18th century, the Evangelical Revival as it later came to be known involved primarily Anglicans, some of whom became Methodists while remaining within the church, others who did not. All of them appear to have found something in evangelicalism that filled a deep spiritual need.

When Matthew Hutton was Archbishop of York in the 1750's he heard with some alarm of the parson of Haworth who had turned a congregation of twelve people into one of at least several hundreds. No lover of 'enthusiasm' the Primate visited this 'hunter of souls' the incumbent William Grimshaw. He asked him to preach on a set text, with two hours preparation.

Grimshaw was convinced that he would be ejected from his living, had his saddle bags packed, and was ready to ride off and join his friends the Methodists. Nevertheless he preached his sermon in his own direct and compelling way, to a receptive audience. The Archbishop was sufficiently impressed to remark that,

'I would to God that all clergy in my Diocese were like this good man.'

The Wesleys and George Whitefield sometimes shared Grimshaw's pulpit where they preached to huge congregations. Across Yorkshire, other less well known parsons also shared their pulpits with popular Methodist preachers. In York, under the very eye of the established church John Wesley

4. Lady Elizabeth Hastings 1682 – 1739

5. John Wesley 1682 – 1739

preached at St. Saviour's church in July 1766, at St Mary's Castlegate and St' Michael's, Spurriergate in June two years later.

This may not have sat well with the church authorities, and it was a further twenty years before Wesley entered another York pulpit. In May 1786 he preached at St Saviour's and St Margaret's and at All Saint's, Pavement in May 1790.

Henry Venn was another notable evangelical Anglican, the son of a man, famous for being the first London clergyman to refuse his pulpit to George Whitefield. He grew up in a household antagonistic to dissent.

Once ordained he began to read seriously and extensively and eventually became aware of a 'sense of sin and a thirst for God, which made him seek in the Bible the Christ who justifies by faith alone'. These were tenets of evangelicalism.

From 1754, he connected with John Wesley attending Wesley's conference at Oxford in 1756. The following year he became an itinerant preacher with George Whitefield, staying at Clifton, the home of The Countess of Huntington.

He became the parson of Huddersfield in 1760. This was the first time that a parish in the industrial West Riding received an evangelical incumbent. His services almost immediately drew large numbers of worshippers. He usually began by reminding the congregation that they were in the presence of the great God of heaven. His sermons were straightforward, explained the scriptures to his audience and were occasionally embellished by racy anecdotes. Locally he became known as 'T'owd Trumpet.'

He was always available to anyone who wished to speak to him. On weekdays he preached eight or ten times in the far reaches of his fairly extensive parish, where he also established class meetings to be held in his absence, along the lines of the Methodists.

He founded what was to become the Elland Club for evangelical clergy in the North of England. They met quarterly at the Huddersfield vicarage for fellowship, the study of the Greek Testament and discussion on a set subject which would make for a more effective ministry. When he left Huddersfield, his successor was unsympathetic, but his former curate George Burnett had become vicar of Elland, and continued his work there.

By 1771, Henry Venn was ill and exhausted, and needed an easier parish. Though his parishioners were deeply upset, and a deputation pleaded with him to stay, offering to pay for another curate to help him, he left for a small rural parish after the Easter of that year.

On handing his parish records to his successor he was asked for an explanation of the description, 'poor' and very poor' against the names of individuals. He replied that he took nothing from the poor, and to the very poor he gave.

His success in Huddersfield had been in the lives he changed at all levels of society, through his preaching and innate goodness. In those years twenty-two men entered the ministry, though some trained at dissenting academies with Venn's blessing.

A likely member of the Elland Club was Richard Conyers, the vicar of Helmsley at the west end of the Vale of Pickering. He was already in the living when he became spiritually awakened. With great zeal and energy he preached, often extempore, every day, every evening and all day on Sunday. He travelled all over his extensive parish, visiting outlying farms and small moorland communities.

The remote chapelry of Bilsdale, though in his parish, had its own curate, William Deason. At the visitation of Archbishop Drummond in 1764 he sourly wrote in his return,

'Mr. Conyers, vicar of Helmsley or his curate, takes the liberty to preach once a fortnight in an old barn, whether licensed or no I cannot tell.'

Richard Conyers made a special effort to reach young people, going from place to place talking and praying with them and their parents.

From the five hundred families within his parish he turned a congregation of forty-five to fifty people into around five hundred. As he himself said,

'Many wicked people were reformed.'

When Henry Venn visited him in 1762, a year when he was quite ill, and probably exhausted, he remarked that vicar Conyers was preaching twenty-one times a week. John Wesley also called on him in 1764, but found him toying with Calvinism. Wesley's preaching seems to have made sufficient impact on him to make him question that area of dogma, at least for a while. It seems likely however, that he eventually settled on the Calvinistic doctrine, as indeed did some of his parishioners.

Wesley found another welcoming pulpit east of Helmsley at Middleton near Pickering, where John King was the very popular evangelical vicar. He combined social work with Godly preaching for about eight years. The following poem was written by one of his parishioners when he was leaving Middleton in 1771 to work his magic on the people of Hull, where his work continued.

'In mournful strains, permit me now to sing,
And vent my sorrows for the loss of King
Unto a fallen, lost and wretched race,
He preached salvation, full and free by Grace
The naked he did clothe, the hungry feed,
He was friend to those who stood in need.'

A few years later a local clergyman, Daniel Duck, received the living of Danby in Cleveland and began a ministry that was to last for forty years. In 1785 he began to keep a journal. One of his early entries records his feelings at the Archbishop's Visitation where he found,

'a great want of zeal and courage and saw the clergy to be in general a dead and loose set of men.'

He had tea with John Wesley and heard him preach several times. He respected and enjoyed the friendship of the local Quakers and Methodists. These latter preached in his church from time to time.

His own preaching rarely satisfied him, but since he recorded 'a throng church' and 'a pretty large congregation' in a church that was sited a long way from most of his parishioners, they presumably did not agree with him. Indeed in 1811 when a Methodist chapel was built at the more central Danby End, one of his admirers wrote a poem explaining it was only his rheumatism which made him attend the 'schism shop' rather than the church. It ends,

'Before my legs began to fail, to church I went in Danby Dale;
And heard with joy our Parson Duck, I cannot now, the worse the luck.'

Such men did immense good within their parishes, but there were not sufficient men of their calibre to continue the work. When Venn left Huddersfield, when Conyers left Helmsley and when King left Middleton, many of their congregations left the church and founded their own Independent chapels. At Danby the Methodists made amazing headway after Daniel Duck died.

The Reverend William Richardson was one of the clergy at York Minster, and shared the opinion of Daniel Duck about many of his colleagues. He preached regularly on his beliefs in the fall of man, redemption by Jesus Christ and justification by faith alone, to 'the great opposition and hostility' of these men. He was fortunate to be supported by the Dean of York who respected his principles and refused to listen to complaints.

He received in August 1772 a letter from his former vicar, who remonstrated with him on his reported tendency to Methodism. He replied,

'Since I went into orders, I have had continued opportunities of observing such deplorable ignorance, such lifeless formality, such shameful immoralities, prevailing among the members of the Established Church as convinced me of the necessity of a general reformation.'

He went on to write that when he first moved to York he found no clergyman there or in the neighbourhood who shared this opinion.

William Richardson, who eventually became head of the Vicars Choral of the Minster, was friendly with, and strongly influenced the Gray family of York. This family, in turn was connected to probably the best known of the secular evangelicals of the later 18th century, William Wilberforce M.P. and anti-slave trader of Hull.

William Gray, a successful lawyer and his wife Faith were active Christians, involved in charity work with likeminded people. William was an almoner for the Wilberforce charities, and helped to administer organisations such as the Church Missionary Society, The Auxiliary Bible Society and the Dispensary and County Hospital

In 1786, with the Rev. Richardson, the Rev. John Grantham and others, William Gray, following an example set by Miss Hill at Tadcaster, founded the first Sunday School in York. He also taught in it and his aims were,

'to promote among the lower classes the knowledge and practice of religious and moral duties.'

All these people and others like them did admirable work during their lifetime, but they remained in the minority of Anglicans during the 18th century. Parts of Yorkshire remained untouched by the Evangelical movement and suffered from a lack of spiritual leadership by the Church of England. Where this was the case it was left to other denominations to supply spiritual sustenance to people clearly in great need of it.

From the time of the Reformation there were English people who felt strongly that the changes made to create an Anglican Church did not go far enough. Initially these people were all lumped together under the derogatory name of Puritans. There were two major groups though these were not always easily distinguishable the one from the other. Neither was there any discernable pattern to the distribution of these dissenting congregations.

6. Independent Chapel Kirkby Moorside North Riding. Built in 1793

Presbyterians had no liturgical or doctrinal problems with the newly established Church of England, but they were against the elaborate ceremony and the Episcopal hierarchy that governed the church. The Presbyterian Church was administered by an assembly of elders with some involvement of the lay congregation. Their ministers were ordained.

Independents placed a greater emphasis on individual spirituality, and answered in all other matters to their own congregations. This emphasis on their own particular church eventually earned them the name Congregationalists.

All Protestant nonconformists were allowed freedom of worship by the Toleration Act of 1698, and the early 18th century saw Dissenting Chapels, being built in Yorkshire, predominantly but not entirely, in the West Riding. They were found in both urban and rural areas, but those which flourished outside of the larger towns were often supported by wealthy patrons.

By 1764 when Archbishop Drummond recorded the Visitation of the Diocese of York there were Presbyterian Meeting Houses at Cottingham, North Ferriby, Nunkeeling and South Cave, as well as at Beverley and Bridlington. Hull which had been pro dissent from the Tudor period had both Presbyterian and Independent Meeting houses.

In the North Riding Presbyterian Meeting Houses were to be found at Aldborough and Great Ayton in addition to the towns of Whitby, Scarborough and New Malton. The Archdeaconry of Richmond, which was in the Diocese of Chester had three small Independent chapels out in the northern Dales.

In contrast, the already more populous and industrialised West Riding, had twenty-seven Presbyterian chapels and eight Independent ones. Among these, Dewsbury and Rotherham had two chapels each; Leeds, Halifax and Sheffield had a chapel of each denomination.

Sheffield probably had the largest dissenting congregation in Yorkshire at their Upper Chapel in Pepper Alley in 1715, when it claimed that 1,163 people attended the services. But the same year saw the death of their pastor Timothy Jollie, and the installation of his successor resulted in the breaking away of about two hundred people to form their own Calvinist Independent Chapel, called Nether Chapel, in Chapel Walk.

The remaining congregation of Upper Chapel, still a large body of people, adopted Unitarian beliefs. This was a trend that was followed by many other Presbyterians, (and a few other Nonconformists) throughout the century, but few if any of them this early.

Unitarianism is the belief in one God, as opposed to the Holy Trinity. It is perceived as an extremely rational form of belief, indeed during the 18th century Unitarians were known as Rational Dissenters.

The two most distinguished Unitarians of the 18th century had strong connections with Yorkshire, but were active well over a generation later than the conversion of Upper Chapel, so clearly there were many others who actively preceded them in the county.

The first 'avowed' Unitarian Congregation in England was founded in London by Theophilus Lindsay, who resigned his living as vicar of Catterick in North Yorkshire to do so. It would seem likely that someone so active in promoting his beliefs had had some success in the north before he left for London.

Joseph Priestley is remembered primarily as a scientist, known for his experiments with gases especially his discovery of oxygen. Born in the parish of Birstall near Leeds in 1733, he was brought up as an Independent. He planned to become a minister, but as he grew older he began to question the tenets of the Calvinistic beliefs he had grown up with. Consequently he chose to go to one of the more liberal Dissenting Academies, since as a nonconformist he could not attend a university.

On leaving the academy he became minister to a poor Independent congregation in Suffolk where he remained for three years. His anti-Trinitarian views eventual made him unpopular and he left for a more welcoming position at Nantwich in Cheshire, to be followed by a spell as a tutor at the Dissenting Academy at Warrington.

By 1767 he was married with a family and moved to Mill Chapel in Leeds as pastor. After a number of years he moved away, but as with Lindsay, his influence must have had an impact on the growth of Unitarianism in Yorkshire.

The move towards a more rational religion ran parallel with increasing respectability of the old dissenting religions. Neither of these held much appeal for the poorer or less educated classes. Lack of fervour saw a decline in numbers at many of these chapels, though not all. But as John Nelson, another native of Birstall wrote to John Wesley'

'Fine preaching does more harm than good here.'

Until the end of the 18th century, Methodists remained within the Anglican Church. John and Charles Wesley, George Whitefield, Benjamin Ingham and other early Methodist evangelists were ordained ministers, though they allowed no parochial boundaries to affect where and when they preached. Where they convinced sufficient people to become members, Societies which required a certain standard of behaviour were formed. In addition to attending religious services where they would hear enthusiastic and charismatic ministers or lay preachers delivering emotionally charged and sometimes life changing sermons and engaging in extempore prayer, Methodists became great singers of hymns. Charles Wesley's many tuneful and much loved hymns along with those of Isaac Watts became an essential and enjoyable part of any Methodist service.

Members were also expected to attend Class meetings once a week. At the Class, ten members and a Class leader prayed together, studied the Bible and discussed religious matters. This discussion could be of a personal nature, and sometimes involved confession of sins. These meetings were regarded as good training for lay preachers and a powerful instrument of evangelism.

Many early Methodists had had little education. Sunday schools which taught literacy and arithmetic were a priority, so that young Methodists would be able to read the Bible, and run the local society. Sometimes there were classes for adults too. Able Society members, often from poor backgrounds benefited and consequently prospered, from learning leadership and administrative skills as well as literacy.

The vicar of Sherburn in the East Riding, in 1764 stated in his visitation return, that there were three Methodist families and some single people in his parish and that they had,

'a licensed meeting house in this parish. They assemble privately three times a week, but are publicly taught by itinerant preachers, sometimes one a week, sometimes one a month, by two or three together of the meanest sort of people.'

Before the Wesley's came north to Yorkshire, Benjamin Ingham had already made some impact in the West Riding. He had been with the brothers when they made their journey in 1735 to Georgia in America.

Like John Wesley, he had met a religious sect, originally from Saxony known as Moravians. Also like Wesley, he was impressed by the way they lived their religion, and on his return to England two years later he joined their brotherhood. This caused a breach with the Wesley's and resulted in Ingham forming his own groups, although he remained on good terms with the Methodists, all his life.

After his marriage to Lady Margaret Hastings in 1741 he went to live at Aberford Hall, from where he went on to evangelise his home county and parts of Lancashire.

Ingham acquired land at Fulneck in the parish of Pudsey in 1744, to assist the Moravian brotherhood establish a settlement. Eventually this community contained a chapel/hall, separate residential accommodation for single men and women, a school and an inn. There was a doctor, a farm, a bakery, a shop, shoe and glove makers and carpenters. These were run for the good of all, not for profit. The ethos of the community was,

'cleanliness and order, of work and godly conversation, of frugal living in surroundings of some grandeur, and above all of stillness.'

The 'grandeur' of the buildings offended Benjamin Ingham, and eventually caused a rift between him and the Moravians. But this was not until several of the religious groups that he established in the West Riding had been taken under the administration of the brotherhood.

From that time, his congregations were known as Inghamites. In 1755 he suggested, at a Methodist Conference that they should amalgamate, but John Wesley was not enthusiastic, and nothing came of it.

About 1760, Ingham became interested in the teachings of two Scottish clergymen, John Glas and Robert Sandeman. These men were former Presbyterian ministers who were excluded from their church for their beliefs, and possibly strange practices. They founded what were really Independent churches, the members being known initially as Glassites, and later as Sandemanians.

Benjamin Ingham sent two of his preachers to observe the Scots in 1761. Their report was clearly favourable, and Ingham joined the sect. This caused some disruption of Ingham's Yorkshire congregations, not all following their leader.

Many joined with the Methodists. At the Visitation of Archbishop Drummond in 1764, York reported one Sandemanian congregation in St Sampson's parish, and there were some people of that persuasion in Birstall, making up a total of 1,700 dissenters in the parish. The chapel at Aberford, where Ingham lived, and one at nearby Tadcaster were referred to as Inghamite chapels, but much of his influence, almost entirely in the West Riding seems to have dissipated by his death in 1771.

Other than the Wesleys themselves, the most influential Methodist in Yorkshire in the early years was John Nelson a stonemason from Birstall, near Leeds. Working in London he heard John Wesley preach and became one of his most active and successful preachers, especially but not entirely in his native county.

By the time that John Wesley visited Birstall in 1742, he found an established society who met in members' cottages or the open air.

By 1750 the congregation was too large to be accommodated inside a cottage. A chapel was built which included a study for small class meetings. The numbers continued to grow and by 1782 the chapel had to be enlarged.

One of the first recorded visits of John Wesley was in 1733. He accompanied his father on a visit to Wentworth House in south Yorkshire, to consult the library of the marquis of Rockingham. The visit went over a Sunday, and he preached in Wentworth church,

'to the no small gratification of the parishioners' he later wrote.

He found a subsequent early visit to south Yorkshire less enjoyable. On his entry into the county between Bawtry and Doncaster, he was quietened by a 'chocksure' [cocksure] fellow who would not allow him to speak. In 1743 he went through Doncaster to Sykehouse, where Methodism first took root in the Doncaster area. In his diary, Wesley wrote,

'I began preaching as soon as I came in and exhorted them to follow after the great gift of God'.

It was a Sykehouse man John Hampson who preached successfully in Doncaster in 1757 and within five years a Society had been formed. The Society flourished and by 1770 John Wesley recorded,

'I rode to Doncaster and preached at noon in the new house, one of the neatest in England. It was sufficiently crowded, and what is more strange, with serious and attentive hearers; what was more unlikely some years since, that such a house, or such a congregation should be seen here.'

Many people who never joined a Methodist Society, often made a considerable contribution to the large congregations and crowds that the Wesleys and their ordained and lay preachers attracted. These people were known as hearers. Some of course, were converted, and in the fullness of time became members. The movement grew ever stronger as the century passed.

Returns for the Visitation of Archbishop Herring in 1743, showed that out of six hundred and forty-five parishes, only twenty-two incumbents mentioned the presence of Methodists in their parish. They were not referred to as dissenters at that time, though many vicars and curates were hostile to them.

Twenty-one years later, the next visitation, by Archbishop Drummond found Methodism well established, particularly in the industrial areas of the West Riding.

There were seventy-one meeting houses, nine hundred and thirty-seven families and countless individuals attending them. These figures would not include the hearers, nor Moravians and members of Inghamite chapels. They were situated in and around Halifax, Leeds, Bradford and Wakefield mainly, with strong outposts in the Sheffield and Doncaster areas.

The North Riding, (the figures excluded the Archdeaconry of Richmond in the north west of the county) had thirty meeting houses, one hundred and five families and one hundred and ninety-six individuals. They were situated throughout the Riding, in Scarborough and Whitby and market towns such as Thirsk, Northallerton, Easingwold and Yarm. Some villages in the Vale of York and the Cleveland area also showed that people in the countryside had been successfully missioned.

The western half of the East Riding along with Beverley was where the Methodist meeting houses were. There were twenty-two, serving eighty-seven families along with forty-three other people. Strangely none were mentioned at Hull or Bridlington which makes for a suspicion that some incumbents more than erred on the side of caution when recording local Methodists.

The Methodists organised themselves on circuits, which, initially took in a large area, and a number of market towns and villages. As numbers grew, so the circuits sub divided. Villages which had a few members but no meeting house, would often encourage good preachers to come and preach in their village.

They were not always well received. In the 1790's Seamer was missioned by a preacher from nearby Scarborough. He received very rough

7. Yarm Wesleyan Chapel North Riding. Built in 1763, John Wesley said it was "by far the most elegant in England."

treatment, at the hands of tenants of Joseph Dennison, encouraged by the steward, a man called Sangster. Sometime later, a second attempt was no more successful, with missiles being thrown at the preachers who eventually had to retreat.

When Joseph Dennison next visited his estates near Scarborough, one of the local Methodists asked to see him, and was cordially received. The result was a piece of land being made available for the first Methodist chapel in the village. Sangster shortly afterwards left Seamer. Wealthy Whigs were generally sympathetic to dissent. And as Earl Fitzwilliam of Wentworth House inferred when questioned about his support for local Methodists on his south Yorkshire estates, he preferred them to be under his eye.

After John Wesley's death in 1791, the Methodists separated from the Church of England. This fact and the reasons for it occasioned much controversy within Methodism and resulted in the first major upset to the Wesleyans. An ordained Methodist minister Alexander Kilham aggressively pushed the separation, and along with six supporters was expelled from the Wesleyan Methodists, as they came to be known.

They formed the Methodist New Connexion, with a membership of about five thousand. Kilham died the following year and William Thom, one of the other six dissidents became their leader. He was a more reasonable man, and despite initial poverty the new denomination flourished, especially in parts of Yorkshire. Within twenty years, Hull had two chapels in that city. The only difference between the two Methodist groups was more lay involvement in the administration of the New Connexion.

Having made such strides during the eighteenth century, it was a foretaste of schisms to come in the following century.

Baptists or as they were often referred to in the 18th century, Anabaptists, were people who believed in adult baptism, as in the New Testament. General Baptists were Arminians, Particular Baptists were Calvinist. Their congregations followed a modified form of Independency which allowed for a loose association of churches. Though there had been small communities of Baptists at Stokesley in the North Riding and Pontefract in the West Riding in the second half of the 17th century, there is little evidence for Baptists in Yorkshire at the beginning of the 18th century.

The first definite information for Baptist congregations come again from opposite areas of the county; Bridlington on the east Coast and Barnoldswick, almost due west from Bridlington, and very near to the Lancashire border.

In 1698 a ship en route for Scotland had to put into Bridlington Bay to ride out bad weather. There were Baptists on board who missioned the town with some success. A small church was built, with an equally small burial ground attached. Robert Prudom became the pastor and John Oxtoby the deacon.

An Oxford graduate George Braithwaite who had become a Baptist convert, was installed as pastor at Bridlington in 1713, where he had a successful ministry which lasted twenty years. During this time he baptised a number of converts from the locality including people from North Burton, Driffield, Flamborough, Hull and Scarborough where churches were formed later in the century.

Towards the end of his time at Bridlington, Pastor Braithwaite published a book entitled 'The Nation's Reproach and the Church's Grief'. This was a hard hitting protest against intemperance. Not surprisingly many of the examples of intemperance that he cited had been witnessed in Bridlington. It seems likely that the book was not well received there, and this may have had something to do with his permanent departure to London shortly after its publication.

There followed a succession of uninspired pastors in the following thirty-four years, but the church survived and indeed helped the formation of a church in Hull in 1736, where two later Baptist churches were subsequently built, at Salthouse Lane in 1755 and George St. in 1794. A church was also established at Bishop Burton in 1764.

Under the leadership of Joseph Gawkrodger, who became pastor in 1767 Bridlington church was re invigorated. He baptised ninety-seven people during his time there.

8. Former Baptist Chapel Great Driffield East Riding. Built 1788 adjacent to burial ground and Beck for baptisms

A number of Bridlington Baptists moved to Driffield in 1786, where at first they held their meetings in the open air. A church was formed the following year and services were held in part of an old brewery. A Mr. Wrightson became pastor in 1788 and shortly afterwards a Meeting House was built. After he resigned in 1795, Driffield was served by ministers from other local baptist churches.

Scottish Baptists founded a church in Beverley in 1791. The first entry from its minute book records,

'This church was originally a branch of the church in Hull'.

The West Yorkshire Baptists owe their origins, for the most part to two cousins. William Mitchel and David Crossley were charismatic presbyterian preachers who were responsible for the existence of twenty Licensed Meeting Houses by 1691.

During a journey to the south of England in 1690, David Crossley met up with some Particular Baptists in Lichfield. These people so impressed him he wrote home,

> 'I will not say I have found men better grounded in the principles of religion than you, neither that I have heard purer doctrine taught than is taught amongst you in none of these societies; but I have found better orders, more godly sincerity, Saint's community and Christian love than with most of you by a great deal; we are much awanting.'

He continued down to London where Independents and Quakers also made a good impression on him, but on his return north it would appear that he had become a Baptist. He settled in Barnoldswick where he established a Baptist Church, whose records date from 1697.

It seems that he convinced his cousin William Michel to become a Baptist too. In his later life Michel moved to Rawdon near Leeds, where a Baptist church was built in 1712. Among their records, an entry reads,

> 'late William Mitchel whose labours were blessed with such agreeable success that many, the first fruits of us, were turned from darkness to light.'

From 1710 to 1720, these early West Riding Baptist Churches were connected to the Rossendale Baptist Church in Lancashire. Congregations were formed at; Cowling Hill (near Barnoldswick), Sutton (near Keighley) in 1711, Gildersome (near Leeds) in 1715, Rodhill End and Stoneslack (in the Huddersfield area) in 1717. Then these churches went on to found other congregations at Gisburn Forest, Salendine Nook in Huddersfield parish, Bradford, Shipley and Halifax, all before 1760.

In the later 18th century missioners from Salendine Nook helped found chapels at Blackley, Pole Moor and Lockwood. Bramley chapel near Leeds was formed as a result of missions from Gildersome. The first Baptist chapel in Leeds itself was founded by Baptists from Bradford, who also helped establish the Farsley church.

By 1764, according to the returns made at Archbishop Drummond's Visitation, there were more than two thousand four hundred Baptists in the West Riding. These were almost entirely from the area west of Leeds to the Lancashire border.

9. Blackley Baptist Church founded in 1789

In the same visitation returns there were very few Baptists found in the North Riding. There was a family in Whitby, another in Hutton Rudby. There was a Licensed Meeting House and six Baptist families at Marton in Cleveland, which is five miles north of Stokesley, and may just be connected to the much earlier Baptist congregation there.

David Fernie became the pastor at Marton about 1780. So successful was he that the congregation grew and a small church was erected there, in which he preached twice every Sunday until 1790. At that time he is believed to have 'sold out' to an Independent minister called Norris.

The Baptists united with the Stockton church in County Durham. By the early 19th century there is no record of either denomination in the village.

William Hague was a Wesleyan from Scarborough who was baptised by Joseph Gawkrodger the Bridlington pastor. He rented a room in Quay St. to use for worship in 1771. Five years later the first Baptist Meeting House was built. William Hague remained pastor there until 1816, much loved and respected. Under his leadership the congregation grew, and the church building had to be extended three times.

The Archdeaconry of Richmond, in the remote north west corner of Yorkshire has no record of Baptist activity until towards the end of the century. Middleham and Wood Hall were missioned from Co. Durham. And a small church established there in 1774.

A Mr. Charles Whitfield, pastor of Hamsterley in Co. Durham was preaching at Wood Hall when he was heard by a watchmaker from Bedale called William Terry. Along with some friends he was converted, and they were baptised. Terry was asked to preach to his Bedale neighbours. This he did with some success, not just in Bedale but at Snape and Masham as well. Eventually in 1793 a church was built, and William Terry continued as pastor there until his death in 1819.

By the end of the century there were significant Baptist ministries in some parts of Yorkshire, but with smaller numbers than other Nonconformist churches, and appear to have relied to a great extent on charismatic preachers.

At the opening of the 18th century the Quakers, as the Society of Friends had come to be known had been established in many parts of Yorkshire for about forty years. The Society was founded by George Fox, a fearless inspirational man who taught that truth was 'to be found in the inner voice of God speaking to the Soul.'

These people had no time for the established church; its ceremony and hierarchy, nor much for other Christian denominations. Quakers were frequently in conflict with both church and secular authorities because of their uncompromising stance on such matters as refusing to swear oaths and refusal to pay tithes and church rates.

Though usually serious and honest of character with a belief in pacifism, in their early years they were often proactive, indeed confrontational when faced with incidents in everyday life which offended them. These activities often ended in unseemly brawls, since non Quakers frequently resented such interference.

One of such incidents was recorded in 1708.

'In the year 1708 there did come a great company of Broad Brims for to stop the May Dance about the pole at Sinnington, and others acting by concert did the like at Helmsley, Kirbymoorside and Slingsby, singing and praying they got them round about the garland pole whilst yet the May Queen was not yet come but when those with flute and drum and dancers came near to crown the Queen the Broad Brims did pray and sing psalms and would not give way while at the finish there was like to be a sad end to the day, but some of the Sinnington bucks did join hands in a long chain and then swept them clean from the pole. At Slingsby there was a great dordum of a fight, but for a great while the Broad Brims have set their faces against all manner of our enjoyment.'

10 George Fox, founder of the Quaker movement. 1624 – 1691

The Toleration Act brought freedom of worship for the Quakers, but alongside this there came a gradual lessening of missioning zeal. Quakers no longer actively sought converts, most new members were born into the Society.

A smaller pool of marriageable members saw a number of Quakers marrying out. Evidence of this can be found in Anglican registers. At Yorkshire ports, Quaker merchants who wished to carry cannon on their ships for protection from piracy also left the Society or were expelled. Along with them were other individuals who were not able to maintain the standards of behaviour required by all Quakers. The result was a decline in numbers through the century.

11 Pickering Friends Meeting House was built in 1793. It originally had its own graveyard, now grassed over

Local Societies were administered by a series of Local, Monthly and Quarterly Meetings. Minutes from these meetings record this decline, as increasingly smaller groups amalgamated.

In the East Riding Kelk had joined Bridlington as early as 1712. Elloughton amalgamated with Cave in 1743, which eventually also absorbed the Beverley Friends. Skipsea and Kilham Local Meetings were dissolved, and by 1773 so was Bridlington. Remaining Quakers from Bridlington joined the Owstwick Monthly Meeting, and about the same time the Cranswick Quakers went to Cave. From their inception, Quakers had always travelled in order to meet together, as numbers declined they had to do so again.

The North Riding Quakers seem to have survived better and for longer than those in the East Riding, but even there the pattern of decline is evident. By 1782 Staintondale Monthly Meeting had closed. Six years later Scarborough and Malton Societies had joined with Pickering, while Thornton Dale was much reduced.

In the Archdeaconry of Richmond in the north west of the county there had been three groups of Quakers in Swaledale, Wensleydale and Richmond. Though some of the remaining records were poorly kept they indicate a declining number of Friends in the area around Healaugh where there was 'less to report' in 1762 and the weekday meeting had a disappointing attendance.

The Swaledale and Richmond Preparatory Meetings joined together in 1785, but there must have been some conflict because by the end of the century the Swaledale Friends met at Reeth.

The West Riding was not only the largest Riding, but was becoming the most populous. In 1764, from the parishes which sent in returns, there were at least five hundred and nineteen Quaker families plus at least a hundred individuals recorded. This compared with two hundred and seventy-five families, (plus those in Richmondshire and Swaledale) in the North Riding and two hundred and two families plus nineteen individuals in the East Riding, indicates where most of the Quakers were to found.

Leeds with fifty-four families, plus numerous Quakers in the surrounding parishes probably saw the greatest concentration. Nearby Bradford had thirty-two families and Wakefield, Huddersfield and Halifax had a respectable number. At Balby near Doncaster in the south of the county where they claim one of the earliest thriving Quaker groups in Britain the numbers had dropped away, Doncaster itself only had twelve families, while neighbouring Rotherham had none.

Sheffield had lost many of its Quakers to the New World at the end of the 17th century, and this may also have affected nearby Rotherham and Doncaster. Nevertheless a Meeting House was built there in 1705, and several notable Quaker families attended. Among those were the Fairbanks, a family of surveyors and Benjamin Huntsman famous for crucible steel.

Once the Society of Friends ceased to confront non Quaker society, they increasingly won respect for their good sense and integrity. Since no official professions were open to them they became more involved in the burgeoning metal, coal extraction and textile industries. They were also in demand as Enclosure Commissioners and official and non-official arbiters in disputes. The testimony to George Hartas of Danby who died in 1835 said,

'His conduct was marked with firm uprightness and integrity…. He sought by many ways to do good to all around him … a man of peace, he was frequently and successfully employed amongst his neighbours in the office of peacemaker.'

Quakers were strong favourers of education for both boys and girls, but were banned from attending the universities. The perceived need for a high quality educational establishment was met when, in 1778, Dr. John Fothergill bought a former foundling hospital at Ackworth in the West Riding, and opened it the following year as a boarding school for Quaker children.

12 Ackworth School

As more Quakers prospered in commerce and industry evidence of their philanthropy and social conscience became apparent. One particularly useful example of this was the founding of an establishment called 'The Retreat' for persons afflicted with disorders of the mind' in York. This was the result of severe treatment resulting in the death of a Quaker patient at another establishment. In its own time 'The Retreat' was perceived as a model for such hospitals and was open to everyone, not just Quakers.

At the beginning of the 18th century England was a protestant country, albeit with several variations on that Protestantism. However there remained a small minority of the population who remained loyal to the Roman Catholic Church.

A high proportion of that minority lived in Yorkshire, mainly on rural estates owned by wealthy Catholics. These people often kept a chaplain to say mass, and educate the local children. Their own sons were often educated abroad. Douai English College in Belgium was one of the preferred colleges used.

Yorkshire Catholics were mainly tolerated, but suffered from exclusion from public life and university education. There were also a number of measures which could result in punitive fines. The Jacobite Rebellions of 1715 and 1745, initiated in Scotland, to put the Catholic Stuart dynasty back on the English throne briefly affected the north of England were exceptions to this toleration. Some local acts of hostility occurred. The Mass House at Stokesley was burnt down.

During the century, which saw land enclosures and industrial growth in the towns, especially the West Riding, some of the rural population moved out of the countryside, including Catholics. It is difficult to estimate how many were living in the larger towns, since the figures we have were usually returns made by Anglican clergy. In Sheffield, where the largest landowner was the Duke of Norfolk, the premier lay Catholic in England, there were two hundred Catholics, who attended the Dukes's private chapel to receive mass, but the visitation return of 1764, records no Catholics in Sheffield at all. There were thirty-three in Hull, but again none were recorded at that visitation.

York was better recorded. During the 18th century the city became a popular social centre. Assembly Rooms were built in 1730. The first grandstand on the Knavesmire Race Course was designed by John Carr in 1754 As a result many wealthy people had town houses and this included Yorkshire Catholic gentry. At the end of the 17th century a boarding school was founded outside Micklegate Bar, for the education of the daughters of Catholic gentry. It is now known as the Bar Convent. In 1699 it also became a free day school.

During the early years of the next century it suffered from some persecution and a chronic shortage of money, but survived. In 1727 a wealthy nun Elizabeth Stansfield put her fortune into the school, and matters improved. By the 1760's Mother Ann Aspinall was able to demolish the original building and employ Thomas Atkinson to design the present Georgian building.

Catholic historian Hugh Aveling tells us that between the 1690's and the 1750's,

> 'Fed by a wave of immigration from declining Catholic country missions, encouraged by the tolerance of the City Council, and sustained by the Bar Convent and the organisation of the two 'parishes' with chapels, the community trebled in numbers.' Though the growth rate slowed down thereafter, by 1791 there were about eight hundred Catholics in the city, 5% of the population.

The last quarter of the century saw the government take measures to lessen the punitive intolerance that had been aimed at Catholics since the Reformation. Known as the Catholic Relief Acts the first was passed in 1778 and allowed the owning of property, the second in 1791 resulted in official tolerance of Catholic worship and schools, and admission to certain legal and military professions.

By 1787, there was a Catholic Northern Vicar Apostolic who had been appointed by Rome to oversee Catholics in the north of England. In that year he reported to the Vatican that in the Diocese of York, (which excluded Richmondshire where there were several Catholic communities.) There were about six thousand, five hundred and ninety-four Catholics out of a population of around four hundred thousand. He thought that the increase in numbers of Catholics was in line with the general increase in population.

The government was worried in the 1790's by events in France. During the French Revolution, many priests fled to England to avoid the 'Terror'. They were welcomed by the authorities, and some settled permanently, a number in Whitby and other places in Yorkshire. They opened schools and convents and worked as priests in the newly built and now acceptable Catholic churches.

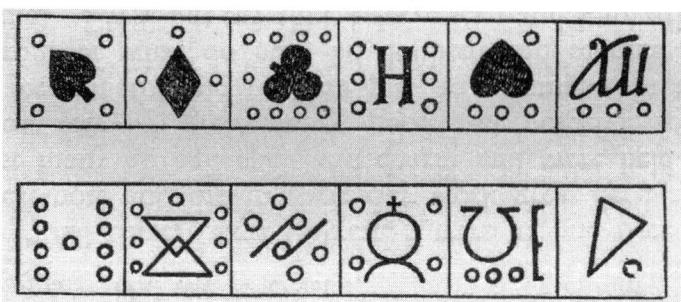

13 Symbols from a 'majic cube' used by the 'witch' Nancy Skaife of Spaunton Moor

A large number of people in Yorkshire did not attend any place of worship even before attendance at the Established Church ceased to be compulsory. This did not mean that they had no belief at all. Many may have believed in a Christian God, but certainly many, including some church and chapel goers, also believed in all manner of supernatural beings and powers.

On the North Yorkshire Moors above Eskdale the Hob, a mischievous and sometimes resident goblin was widely believed in.

Peter Appleton from Fryup, when an old man in the mid 1800's said that when he was a child, he and others played on Fairy Cross Plain. They amused themselves by running round the rings there, always careful not to run nine times around because that would have given the fairies power over them.

The law against witchcraft was repealed in 1736, but there is plenty of evidence to suggest that belief in them continued throughout the century and beyond. Canon John Atkinson of Danby wrote about Nan Hardwick, who was born in 1765. There were many tales about her including her changing shape when she was chased by a group of youths.

Molly Cass of Leeming was another such. She was believed to fly on a broomstick. One time she was ducked nine times in Bedale Mill Dam.

These beliefs were not confined to the countryside. Mary Bateman, who lived at the end of the 18th century came from Topcliffe, but became notorious in Leeds. For her, charms were not enough. She was proved guilty of using poison on her victims and was hanged for murder at York in 1809.

Witchcraft could be good or bad. The antidote to malignant witches was the 'wise man'. He was consulted by people who thought they had been bewitched by black magic. He was also believed to be able to deal with a variety of other problems such as finding lost or stolen property and brewing herbal remedies and potions. White witches did much the same.

Master Sadler was a wise man from the Bedale area. He advertised his services in 1773, promising to cure 'ague'. He did this by writing the sufferer's name on the back of his fireplace and reciting a special incantation.

All these beliefs had existed from time out of mind and were still much in evidence in the 18th century. The increase in education and the growth of the evangelical Christian movement began to check them to some extent, mainly in the urban areas. In the rural areas they continued to be accepted usually running alongside a genuine belief in a Christian God, sometimes not.

The most important factor in religion during the 18th century was the advent and growth of the Evangelical Movement.

Untouched by this movement were the Roman Catholics, who maintained their numbers throughout the century, in line with the general increase in population. Their clergy were carefully watched and any indication of missioning zeal would have had adverse consequences, except perhaps in York.

The Quakers, sometimes strident and aggressive at the beginning of the century became quieter as the 18th century progressed. They lost many members as Friends married out, or failed to conform to the strict rules of behaviour the Society was bound by. Monthly Meetings closed or amalgamated and rural Quakers once again had to travel many miles to their Meeting House.

This movement did not affect everyone in Yorkshire, not even every Christian. Most members of the Anglican clergy resisted its momentum. Many small country parishes, where there were few if any freeholders, and the parson was supported by the landowner, were no-go areas. Anyone preaching with enthusiasm in the open air in such villages could be met with hostility and occasional violence.

14 Methodists preached in the open air

Evangelicalism resulted in a diversity of belief and ministry which remains within the Established Church to this day. In the 18th century it resulted in areas which had evangelical clergy also enjoying a more energetic and spiritually engaged church.

Without question the Wesley brothers, George Whitefield and other early Methodist leaders started a movement of such enormous impact that it transformed the lives of hundreds of people in Yorkshire, especially the poorest.

By addressing crowds in the open air, by encouraging their religious fervour through the singing of Charles Wesley's melodic hymns, by organising Sunday schools and Bible study classes, by encouraging and facilitating literacy and Bible reading, indeed Bible ownership, the Methodists and other evangelicals moved together to create a religious force that was to gather strength up to and into the 19th century. Yorkshire was a county where they had their greatest early success, and where they brought joy and hope to many whose lives had been miserable and hopeless.

BIBLIOGRAPHY

C. Annesley & P. Hoskins. Archbishop Drummonds Visitation Returns 1764. 1 Borthwick Texts and Calenders 21. York, 1997.

C. Annesley & P. Hoskins. Archbishop Drummonds Visitation Returns 1764. 11 Borthwick Texts and Calenders 23. York, 1998.

C Annesley & P. Hoskins. Archbishop Drummonds Visitation Returns 1764. 111 Borthwick Texts and Calenders 26. York, 2001.

J.C. Atkinson. Forty Years in a Moorland Parish London, 1891.

H. Aveling. Northern Catholics. London, 1966.

F.L. Cross (ed.) The Oxford Dictionary of the Christian Church. London, 1957.

F. Crowder & D. Greene. Rotherham. Wakefield, 1971.

P. Crowther. Witchcraft in Yorkshire. Clapham, 1973.

R. Davies. Methodism. London, 1963.

R. Fieldhouse & B.Jennings A History of Richmond & Swaledale. Chichester, 2005.

E. Gray. The Papers and Diaries of a York Family 1764 -1839. Sheldon Press, 1967.

B.D.J. Harrison & G. Dixon (eds.) Guisborough Before 1900. Guisborough, 1982.

S. Harrison. The History of Driffield East Yorkshire. Pickering, 2002.

D. Hey. Yorkshire From A.D.1000. London, 1986.

D. Hey. A History of Sheffield. Lancaster, 1998.

D. Hey. "The Changing Pattern of Nonconformity 1660-1851", Essays in the Economic and Social History of South Yorkshire S. Pollard & C. Holmes eds. Sheffield, 1976.

T Hinderwell. The History and Antiquities of Scarborough and the Vicinity. York, 1811.

N.A. Hudleston. History of Malton and Norton. Scarborough, 1962.

J, Lythe. Early Methodism in York. York, 1985.

J. McDonell. (ed.)A History of Helmsley Rievaulx and District. York, 1953.

D. Neave. Port, Resort and Market Town, A History of Bridlington. Hull, 2000.

F.S. Popham (ed.) A History of Christianity in Yorkshire. Surrey, 1954.

A. Rowntree (ed.)The History of Scarborough. Letchworth, 1931.

J. Rushton. The History of Ryedale. Pickering, 2003.

I. Sellars (ed.) Our Heritage The Baptists of Yorkshire, Lancashire and Cheshire 1647-1987. Leeds, 1987.

M. Walton. Sheffield, It's Story and It's Achievements. Sheffield, 1949.

F. Wrigley. The History of the Yorkshire Congregational Union. London, 1923.

CHAPTER 2

RELIGION IN YORKSHIRE IN THE NINETEENTH CENTURY

Among other parts of England, Yorkshire saw a large increase in population during the 19th century, and was one of the counties affected by burgeoning industry. From the 1840's the spread of the railway made movement of people and goods quicker and easier than ever before, bringing rural workers into the expanding cities and holidaymakers to the coastal and inland resorts.

Leeds was the most populous of the Yorkshire towns. By the middle of the century it had one hundred and seventy-two thousand, two hundred and seventy people. It was followed by Bradford, Halifax, Huddersfield and Sheffield, all in the West Riding. Hull with almost eighty-five thousand people was the only sizeable town in the East Riding, and in the North Riding, Scarborough was the largest with only twelve thousand, six hundred and fifteen residents.

At the beginning of the century, the government introduced a census of the population, which was taken every ten years from 1801, and which increased in remit almost every decade. In 1851, they also took a census of Religious Worship. This required every congregation of whatever denomination to make a return of information which included among other things the following particulars. The size of and accommodation provided by the premises, both rented and free seats, as well as standing room, whether the denomination had sole use of the building and when it was built, if after 1800. Particularly interesting was the number of people who attended worship at all services on 30th March, and the number of Sunday school scholars attending

It is not possible to tell how many people went to more than one service, or how many attended because they had been encouraged to do so on that particular day. Nor can we know exactly how accurate the figures returned were, especially as many appear to have been rounded up. But it is generally accepted that they were sufficiently accurate to present a true state of religion in Britain in the middle of the century.

The most striking fact to emerge from the religious census was that when compared with the population figures provided by the ordinary census, it was obvious that about half the population attended no religious service at all.

15 Industrialised Bradford in the nineteenth century

Thomas Hebblethwaite a literate labourer of West Ayton in the North Riding, wrote about village life in the 1830's, and commented,

> 'The Sabbath Day too was not held in such respect as it is today. The game known as 'fiveballs' being constantly played every Sunday weather permitting on the end of the house known as the Forge Valley Hotel, ...and though one of the magistrates constantly passed them so employed I never heard that he even remonstrated with them. ...other games such as pitch and toss going on at the time unreproved, nay even tolerated.'

He was writing at the end of the century, and clearly thought respect for religion had improved.

Throughout the 1800's, if the articles and correspondence in the newspapers were any indication, interest in religion was enormous. Argument over theology, doctrine and ritual became a popular pursuit among the literate, and the press was the medium used.

Such was the interest that several newspapers made a serious attempt to repeat the religious census thirty years after the original. By that time it was obvious that the government had no inclination to repeat the survey made in 1851.

The Yorkshire towns covered by the 1881 'census' were Sheffield, Rotherham and Barnsley in the West Riding, Hull in the East Riding and Scarborough in the North Riding. The following appeared in the Scarborough Mercury on Saturday, 10th December 1881,

'On Sunday last, a census was taken of the attendance at all the places of worship in Scarborough. It was done at our instigation, and the arrangements for it were made by us. Every care was taken to secure the nearest possible approach to absolute accuracy. Circulars were sent to the leading clergymen and ministers connected with every place of worship in the borough, inviting their co-operation and assistance. In almost every instance this was cordially rendered, and printed forms were forwarded to be filled up in each case by some person in authority. In the very few instances in which the co-operation of the officials could not be obtained, enumerators were specially appointed to count the number of persons present. The returns duly arranged and tabulated will be found below.'

If the other newspapers were as thorough as the Scarborough Mercury, there is no reason to doubt that the statistics taken in 1881 were at least as accurate as those returned in 1851.

The number of 'censuses' taken in 1881 were too few and unrepresentative for any definite conclusions to be drawn from the figures, but a couple of tendencies were apparent. The first was that the majority of people were attending a service in the evening, whereas in 1851 most people had gone to church in the morning. Secondly and more interesting was the fact that although attendances at all the places of worship had increased phenomenally, they had only kept pace with the increase in population. Indeed, it is possible that they had lost some ground.

Mr. W. T. Adey, a member of the Scarborough Baptist congregation calculated the statistics from his own church's figures,

'In 1851, there were in the borough 500 worshippers (morning and evening); in 1881, 671; showing a gain of 171 or 34 per cent., whilst the population has increased from 12,844 to 30,236, or 136 per cent.' He concluded that there was still more work to be done.

The dawn of the 19th century saw the Church of England or Anglican Church seeking desperately to retain its grip on the nation's religion, as the Methodists went from strength to strength. The Evangelical Revival of the previous century had resulted in more spiritually active, caring and enthusiastic clergy within the Anglican Church, and within some of the old dissenting denominations such as the General Baptists and Independents, (also known as Congregationalists) but the greatest impact by far was made by the followers of John and Charles Wesley.

16 Saint Peter's Helperthorpe, East Riding. Built by the Sykes family of Sledmere in 1871 and extended in 1893, it is one of the many "Sykes" churches built in villages where there was previously no church

While John Wesley lived, the Society remained within the Church of England, but shortly after his death in 1797, they became an independent denomination. Clearly efforts had to be made to remedy the failings that the Establishment could see were aggravating the situation.

Some Anglican churches that had been too small, were rebuilt, or enlarged, and provided some free seating for the poor. The means to do this came from both public and private sources. In the East Riding, the Sykes family of Sledmere, built a number of small village churches on their large estates, where no church had been. Other landowners did much the same, though on a smaller scale. It took time to pass the various Acts of Parliament to make the money available, but by the 1820's building started and continued throughout the century.

The improved churches were an attempt to keep up with the increasing population. This they barely achieved. These churches were found in large towns, principally but not entirely the industrial ones, and in the vast upland rural parishes where there was clearly a demonstrable absence of Anglican accommodation.

The livings of poor parishes continued to be augmented, and efforts were made to ensure every parish had a resident clergyman. Success was limited. In Huntington, near York, as late as 1850, on the death of their non-resident vicar of twenty-five years, the parishioners delivered a petition by hired cab to the Archbishop at Bishopthorpe Palace pleading for a resident clergyman.

Most important was the increasing number of evangelical clergymen, often charismatic preachers who were greatly loved by their parishioners.

> 'At that time we had the best of vicars, an Evangelical gentleman who took his utmost pains for the spiritual and moral welfare of our villages. Though his services were not appreciated as they ought to have been. A very charitable man too, dispensing his charities alike to Nonconformist as to members of his own church, as he had not the least taint of bigotry about him.'

So wrote the West Ayton labourer, George Hebblethwaite of the vicar of Seamer.

In Wakefield between 1801 and the 1820's, in addition to the parochial clergy, an evangelical Anglican preacher, Thomas Rogers had a lectureship. His sermons were given in the evenings, in the parish church to his large congregations. He emphasised piety within the family, encouraging daily family prayers. He was even credited by some with an improvement in the atmosphere and behaviour in Wakefield town.

17 Saint Stephen Anglican "low" church Fylingdales North Riding. Built 1821 it is a fine example of an evangelical "preaching" church with large pulpit

It was particularly important that the quality of the Anglican clergymen was equal to that of their dissenting rivals. In the Diocese of York the demand for new clergymen was greater than provision by the universities. One answer to this problem was the ordination of non-graduate 'literate' young men. The first quarter of the 19th century saw the largest number of non-graduates in the Diocese. Archbishop Vernon Harcourt turned to his evangelical clergy to help rectify the shortage by preparing a number of these 'literate' men for ordination.

Samuel Knight whose father had been an ex coal miner and dissenting minister had attended Magdalene College Cambridge, courtesy of the evangelical Elland Society. He became the first incumbent of the newly built Holy Trinity Church, Halifax in 1798, and he took pupils as did his son James.

There was some controversy concerning the ability of these non-graduate clergy, but in the 1819 'Gentleman's Magazine' a contributor wrote,

> 'His Grace of York has oftener than once been pleased to say, that, generally speaking he has found the non-graduate clergy to make the most exemplary parish priests.'

The increasing amount of Anglican Church reform in the first half of the 19th century gradually began to make a clerical career more attractive. Augmentation of livings and regulation of stipends, plus the emergence of two more universities, along with an increase in Anglican colleges saw the end of the privately prepared, potential incumbents.

The years when such young men studied and were influenced by good, evangelical clergymen across the county, helped to promote the evangelical cause for a further generation, and at a time when it was once again under attack. How many of their successors shared their piety and commitment is debateable.

A good example of an Anglican cleric of the period who was not an evangelical, was the famous Reverend Sydney Smith, rector of Foston, a parish just north of York. This Oxford educated, gentleman was better known for his wit than his piety. His preferred profession was the law, to which he was eminently well suited, but his father refused to support him in this, and he settled on being a clergyman.

Sydney Smith, though not wealthy, had many friends who were both rich and influential at a national level. Consequently he was well received into the Anglican circle in York which centred around the Archbishop. An educated man, he was in demand socially. Nevertheless he put his energies into his life as the rector of Foston. He was involved in running the glebe farm, and acted as a local doctor and occasional teacher.

18 Sydney Smith 1771 – 1845

His personal religious beliefs were very straightforward, and he had little time for discussing the minutiae of theology. He accepted the doctrines of the Anglican Church unquestioningly, and had a strong dislike of both Dissent and Roman Catholicism. He was however implacably opposed to any kind of persecution of others for their beliefs. 'Tolerance of opinion and courtesy to individuals was his firm rule.'

His sermons were 'vivid, homely and humane.' He was a good representative of the large numbers of Anglican clergymen who had little time for the evangelicals within his church and without, and who, when Anglo Catholicism emerged in the 1830's, had no interest in their extremes either. Later such men were described as belonging to a 'broad church'.

The 1830's saw the beginning of the 'Oxford Movement', so called because its origins were associated with the university there. The leaders of the movement, men such as John Henry Newman, John Keble, and Edward Bouverie Pusey, believed that the Church of England had become too 'plain' and that there was too much liberalism in its theology.

They postulated a 'Branch Theory' which stated that Anglicanism along with Roman Catholicism and Orthodoxy formed three branches of the one 'Catholic Church'. They wanted to see a revival of traditional aspects of the liturgy. As the movement grew in strength it began to influence both the theory and practice of Anglicanism. It led to the terms 'High' church and 'Low' church being used to differentiate between a church run on Anglo Catholic lines and one run in the more simple evangelical tradition.

High Church clergymen made a greater use of vestments. Choirs were formed. The Eucharist became more important in worship. Churches were highly decorated. Statues, crucifixes, candles and incense were also introduced.

Robert Wilberforce, son of the famous abolitionist studied at Oxford where he became connected with the Anglo Catholic Movement, and friendly with Newman, Keble and Pusey. He became Archdeacon of the East Riding and used his influence to promote his beliefs which were so strong, that after the death of his second wife, he converted to Catholicism. He was training to become a priest when he died in Rome in 1857

One of the first Yorkshire churches to have an Anglo Catholic vicar was Leeds in 1837. The advowson of St Peter's Church was in the gift of twenty-three trustees. A majority of sixteen men were impressed by the reputation of Walter Farquhar Hook as a preacher, and for his care of and generosity to his parishioners, and supported his appointment. In other eyes this did not compensate for his High Church beliefs and he experienced some opposition. Wanting robes for his choristers, he had to pay for them himself.

Despite Leeds being an area where the Methodists and other evangelical congregations flourished, he was very successful in drawing large attendances to hear his sermons. During his incumbency the number of his communicants rose tenfold. In 1851 the evening congregation in his church was two thousand eight hundred, and it was not unusual for there to be more people than seats. He felt strongly that all church seating should be free, and set about to make this happen in his churches.

41

19 The Pulpit at South Cliff Church, Scarborough with panels by Rossetti

Leeds parish contained a large number of chapels of ease. Rev. Hook kept control of fourteen of these chapelries in order to find,

> 'some place for persecuted High Churchmen to flee into.'

A reference to the fact that over two centuries of anti-Catholic feeling, still made the public at large antagonistic to anything that hinted of Catholicism.

A new church was built on the south cliff at Scarborough in 1863. The interior of this church was highly decorated by Pre Raphaelite artists, and had colourful stained glass windows. The undoubtedly 'High' church was consecrated with much ceremony, which provoked a certain amount of controversy. A doggerel verse entitled 'Church in the Lurch' was circulated, containing lines such as,

> 'Where grass green pulpits blazing,
> With Popish saints amazing,
> And sheeted lads in chorus,
> With Popish chants will bore us.'

The decoration on the pulpit was so 'Catholic' it had to be covered up for years.

In the parish of Helmsley, Charles Norris Grey became vicar in 1870. An indomitable High Churchman, a son and grandson of bishops, he had a private income and feared no man. He waged war on every branch of non-conformity, but could ally himself with protestant dissenters against the local Roman Catholics. Given his beliefs, this seems strange, but when some of his friends from Oxford eventually converted to Catholicism, he directed his not inconsiderable disgust at them too.

He was careful not to make too many changes immediately, but one of the first things he did was start a parish magazine, one of the earliest in the country. This publication was wide in its remit. It not only covered parish affairs, but dealt with social problems, health and hygiene matters, and carried rebukes to anyone the vicar felt needed them, including the Earl of Feversham his patron, and the Archbishop of York.

He introduced modest ritual in his services at first, but in 1879 he established the Choral Eucharist which became one of the essential features of Helmsley church worship. Soon colour was in evidence and a little later incense was used. Copes were worn in 1881 and soon all manner of vestments became the norm. These Anglo Catholic features were always explained to the parishioners from the pulpit, in the school and in the parish magazine. They were not however accepted without comment or indeed resistance. Many parishioners took offence at the introduction of confession, and the Sisterhoods, i.e. Anglican nuns, who, funded by the vicar, worked in the parish.

His greatest contribution to the Oxford Movement was initiating a series of retreats at Helmsley, where High Church clergy came from all over England for a four day stay. He persuaded eminent clergy such as Dr. King, Bishop of Lincoln, The Rev. S. Coles, President of Pusey House, Oxford, Canons Newbolt, Brady and Scott Holland, Tractarians all, to conduct these.

Baptists, Presbyterians and Independents were the denominations that from the Reformation onwards had refused to worship within the Established Church. In the 17th and 18th century it was not always easy to differentiate between the latter two groups. They were both Calvinist in doctrine; that is they believed in the predestination of souls to either heaven or hell. Calvinists belonged to the 'elect'. They were destined for heaven no matter how they lived their lives.

The Baptists believed in adult baptism. The original Confession of Faith by one of their earliest leaders, John Smyth stated,

20 Horkinstone Baptist Chapel - Oxenhope

'The Church of Christ is a company of the faithful, baptized after confession of faith and of sins, which is endowed with the Power of Christ…. Baptism is the external sign of the remission of sins, of dying, and of being made alive, and accordingly does not belong to infants.'

They were Arminian in doctrine, which held that true Christian repentance of sin, no matter how heinous that sin, brought God's Grace and salvation. Before the 19th century some Baptists became Calvinists and left the General Baptists. They called themselves Particular Baptists.

In the 18th century Yorkshire Baptists had established themselves in the area of the West Riding around Leeds, Bradford and Huddersfield, and in the western Dales. To a lesser degree, they made some impact in the East Riding and at the coastal resorts of Bridlington and Scarborough. By the 1820's there was a small group of Baptist churches in Richmondshire. No great impact was made in the rest of the North Riding.

The General Baptists became involved in the Evangelical Revival. The more enthusiastic of them broke away from the main group, and called themselves the Baptist New Connexion. The churches were independent until 1813 when the Baptist General Union was formed for mutual guidance and support. The Particular Baptists remained aloof from this and stayed exclusive.

The Evangelical Revival saw the Baptists make headway, but mainly in the towns. There had not been any Baptists in the south of the county, but the

44

first half of the 19th century saw nine churches built. Doncaster had a Baptist church by 1849, and in 1851 there were two Baptist churches and four schools in Sheffield, and two churches in Rotherham. Barnsley and Penistone had also been successfully missioned.

The Particular Baptists however were the most successful of all the Baptist churches in Yorkshire. In the areas in and around Leeds, Bradford, Huddersfield and the Dales, they held most of the churches recorded in the census of religion. The difference was much the same in the other Ridings, but on a smaller scale.

West Riding 1851	Number of churches	Morning attendance
Particular Baptist	71	14,568
General Baptist	5	643
Baptist New Connexion	15	3,058
Baptist (undefined)	7	363
Scotch Baptist	1	35

The most important and successful place in the North Riding for Baptists was Scarborough, which had been missioned from Bridlington in the 18th century, and where it went from strength to strength. Though there was a church at Malton by the middle of the century, there is no other indication that the Scarborough Baptists had successfully spread the word beyond that town.

The only other indication of evangelical success was at Northallerton and the adjacent large village of Brompton, where two churches were erected in the second quarter of the century. There had been two Baptist churches at Aiskew, in the parish of Bedale, and one each at Crakehall and Masham, in the 1820's, also at Richmond. By mid-century the Richmond, Masham and Crakehall congregations had gone.

In the middle of the 19th century four of the fourteen Baptist churches in the East Riding were in Hull, two in Beverley, and one each in Bridlington, Driffield, Bishop Burton, Hedon, Hutton Cranswick and Kilham. Eleven of these were Particular Baptists, two unspecified Baptists and one Scottish Baptist church. Before the century was out, at least three of the remainder ceased to function. At Brandesburton and Hunmanby they sold their buildings to the Methodists. Skidby Baptist Church established in 1819 as a result of the evangelical missioning movement seems not to have lasted until mid-century, and by 1892 was an 'unpicturesque ruin'.

The Baptists continued to increase their congregations in line with the increasing population, but made no further inroads into the East Riding. Clearly Baptists had some appeal for townspeople, and tradesmen in larger villages, but did not make much impact on smaller communities.

The most successful of the Old Dissenting congregations throughout the 19th century were the Independents. They were autonomous and by the 19th century they were also known as Congregationalists.

Like the Presbyterian and Unitarian churches they appealed mostly to the middle classes and were rarely to be found in sparsely populated rural areas. Most large towns and market towns in Yorkshire had at least one Congregational chapel. Places such as Hull and Leeds often had more than one. They continued in this way throughout the century, in spite of missioning less affluent areas. As late as 1894, T Nicholson, president of the Yorkshire Congregational Union said,

> 'As Congregationalists we must get rid of the limited idea that ours is a mission merely to the middle class... The balance of power has shifted.'

Many long established congregational churches had endowments which ensured their continued existence. Most members of the congregations were financially secure. Some such as Sir Titus Salt were extremely rich and used their wealth to further Congregationalism. When new areas were missioned these circumstances did not always apply, and new churches could fail through lack of money.

Strangely York was the one large town where Old Dissent had not flourished. Baines 1823 Directory tells us,

> 'The Independents though formerly scarcely known in York, have of late become a numerous body, and will probably under the ministry of the zealous and eloquent young preacher, lately called to preside over them, still further increase. Their chapel......called Lendal chapel was built in the year 1814, at a cost of £3,000, and will accommodate a congregation of 1,000 persons.' In addition to the three Sunday services there was a lecture on Thursday evenings and a prayer meeting on Monday evenings.

Another striking exception was Swaledale in the western half of the North Riding. There the Congregationalists enjoyed some success during the early part of the century as a result of the Evangelical Revival.

The small market town of Reeth whose Congregationalist church had been established in 1783, hosted a large evangelical meeting in 1803. It must have impacted on the local people, because a church was opened at Low Row about four miles west of Reeth in 1808. This group appears to have struggled between 1825 and 1835, when it amalgamated with Reeth. In the mid-century, it was functioning again when the Rev. Thomas College was appointed pastor. He was described as, 'of a highly pleasing nature'. The next year the young pastor declared',

> 'There is no station that stands more in need of a Home Missionary than Reeth, the whole district for many miles around being in an awful state of spiritual and moral wretchedness.'

It seems possible the young pastor had problems with his flock, and was no longer of a 'pleasing nature' to some of them, and a schism occurred. There were two Congregational groups at Low Row in 1851. One had an attendance of forty-six adults   and forty-eight Sunday school pupils. The other saw thirty-three people at their chapel on census Sunday.

In Richmond a chapel had been built in 1835. It had a congregation of about sixty in 1851, but when a West Riding Missionary Society visited it fifteen years later, they found the church neat and clean, but there was no pastor. There were still however,

> 'some true hearted Christian disciples, among them a few Godly women.'

Though fiercely independent in all ways, the Congregational churches of the West Riding formed an association in 1819. The aims were purely evangelical, and initially were successful, but enthusiasm was waning by 1849. The association found it was mainly helping struggling congregations with donations of money. Batley, Harrogate, Lightcliffe and Elland all benefited that year. At Morley,

> 'where the incorruptible seed continues to be sown.' A donation of £40 was made.

The North Riding churches formed their association in 1823 in Pickering, which had a long tradition of Independency. This group was responsible for churches being established at Guisborough, Mickleby, Northallerton, Easingwold and Rillington in the East Riding. Later in the century they had some success at Robin Hoods Bay, the developing resort of Redcar and the new industrial town of Middlesbrough.

The strength of the East Riding association was in Hull. It missioned a wide rural area mostly within a radius of twenty-five miles of the city. Nafferton, Patrington, Brandesburton and Thorngumbald failed but the other

21 The Congregational Church, Swanland, East Riding. The Centre was built in 1804 and the wings added in 1854

churches at Pocklington and Elloughton survived and rebuilt or enlarged their premises in the second half of the century.

By the beginning of the 19th century most Presbyterian churches had become Unitarians, or ceased to exist at all. The 1851 religious census gave two Presbyterian churches in the West Riding, and one each in the North and East Ridings.

The Unitarians did not have an easy time establishing themselves, indeed they were not a legal denomination until 1813. Their beliefs were very different from all the other relatively orthodox Christians. Their theology rejects the doctrine of the Trinity and the divinity of Jesus in favour of belief in a single God. They have no formal creed.

Unitarians placed great emphasis on the intellect and had a strong belief in individual liberty. They were also known as Rational Dissenters, and were not disconcerted, unlike many Christians, by the Darwinian theory of evolution. Indeed they embraced it, along with most subsequent scientific discoveries.

Like the Congregationalists, their appeal was to the wealthy middle classes. Greatest success came in the West Riding, where most of the Presbyterian churches had been. By 1851 they had seventeen churches there, but only three in the North Riding and two in the East Riding.

About the middle of the century, one of these was briefly at Elleker, where a Methodist, having had a disagreement with his own church, decided to try the Unitarians, which had a membership of six people. He did not go many times before he returned to the Methodists. He commented,

> 'There's nowt for a poor sinner at that shop: no Saviour to die for him, and no Holy Ghost to renew him. The Bible is vary lahtle better than an old song; as for heaven, they're not quite sure about that! Ah can doo as weel wi'out that religion as wiv it.'

Nevertheless, to a limited number of people it had its appeal, and churches continued to be opened throughout the century.

Though there was no great local demand for one, a Unitarian church was opened at Scarborough in 1877, mainly it was believed to cater for visitors to the town. But in December 1881, Scarborough Unitarians had a congregation of fifty-nine in the morning and fifty-eight in the evening. This at a time of year when there were very few visitors.

Members of the Society of Friends, often known as Quakers belonged to a radical Christian movement with strong principles and modes of behaviour and speech. Founded by George Fox, they withstood considerable persecution during the later 17th century.

The 18th century saw them maintain their quaint speech and dress, and above all their integrity, but also withdraw into a period of 'quiet' which allowed a cessation of evangelical missioning for converts, at a time when other protestant churches were very active, and when the Methodist movement became established. The membership dropped considerably during the century.

In 1791 the Yearly Meeting issued a list of 'Queries' to establish that the various local groups, known as Preparative Meetings, were keeping to the spirit and rules of the Society. The returns were to be made by the Monthly Meetings. They enquired about attendance, setting a good example, reading the scriptures, avoiding 'vain spats' and excessive gaming and drinking among other things. There were questions as to their business dealings, and whether they were paying their taxes and whether they admonished members who wished to marry non-Friends.

The answers to these have survived for the Leeds Monthly Meetings from 1809 to 1849 and give a flavour of early 19th century Quakerism. Referring to attendance, Meetings were almost always well attended on Sunday mornings, less so in the afternoon and midweek. It was admitted that

22 Joseph Rowntree 1801 – 1859

there was some drowsiness during the meetings and that 'there is not much growth in the Truth'. Some 'attenders' were also present at meetings, and were described as 'serious' or 'well-disposed persons', but few had joined the Society. Membership was a continuing cause for concern.

On the North Yorkshire Moors in 1793, the small market town of Kirbymoorside together with the nearby village of Hutton Le Hole had one hundred and two Quaker members. By 1851 the Hutton meeting had been given up, and only eleven Friends attended the Kirbymoorside Meeting on that census Sunday morning.

The reasons for this loss of membership were various. Some Quakers emigrated to America. Friends involved in merchant shipping to and from the Yorkshire Coast offended against Friends' pacifist beliefs by carrying guns on their ships to deter pirates, and were consequently disowned by the Society. The most consistent reason was 'marrying out', an act which also meant disownment.

While small in numbers, Quakers were well regarded by non-Quakers because of their honesty and integrity. They were called on to act as arbiters in various disputes, and were frequently used as enclosure commissioners and in other matters where impartiality was necessary. Their good standing and influence in the community increased as Friends entered public and political life in the 19th century, to a level not reflected in the size of the Society.

The Rowntree family of York, one of the best known Yorkshire Quaker families established a grocery business in 1822. This formed the basis for the very successful cocoa and chocolate business which provided money for charitable works on a grand scale. To this day the name is synonymous with work on behalf of the underprivileged, and the monitoring of social abuse of many kinds.

Among the many kinds of public spirited enterprises undertaken by Friends was an interest in furthering education, not only of their own children, but those of non-Friends of the poorer classes. They had been well to the fore in the establishment of Sunday Schools from which developed 'Adult Schools', which really took off in the 1840's. Though only a minority of these adult learners ultimately joined the Society of Friends, they must have been strongly influenced by them, and it was at least one way to increase membership in a discouraging period.

The 1851 census returns in the East Riding were dire, with only three Meeting Houses, and a total morning attendance of one hundred and thirty people. The equally rural North Riding had seventeen Meeting Houses and a total morning attendance of four hundred and eight people. The highly populated West Riding contained thirty-five Meeting Houses which had seen an attendance of two thousand, one hundred and ninety people. Not all these need have been members, since there were often some 'attenders' there.

The next few years saw controversy between those Quakers who wished to abolish the stipulation that marrying-out meant disownment, and those who wished to maintain the status quo. In 1859 John Stephenson Rowntree, wrote of one Yorkshire Monthly Meeting where, between 1837 and 1854, sixty-one members had married out, and consequently had to leave the Society. He continued,

'Surely ecclesiastical history does not present a more palpable case of failure, in endeavouring to attain a desirable end through wrong means.'

In that year, 1859, the reformers won. By the 1880's half of all Friends were marrying outside their faith.

Following this reform, in 1860 Friends were no longer obliged to wear 'plain dress' and use 'plain speech', mainly the use of 'thou' and 'thee', and the easing of some of the more stringent requirements for membership of the Society of Friends seems to have had good results. Membership of Yorkshire Friends at the Quarterly Meeting in 1862 was two thousand and sixty-nine. By 1902 it had risen by thirty-three per cent. These Yorkshire figures were fifteen percent of the national membership

On 24th May 1738, John Wesley, an Anglican cleric had an experience he described thus,

'In the evening I went ...to a society in Aldersgate St. where one was reading Luther's preface to the Epistle to the Romans. About a quarter before nine, while he was describing the change which God works in the heart through faith in Christ, I felt my heart strangely warmed. I felt I did trust in Christ, Christ alone, for salvation; and an assurance was given me that He had taken away my sins, even mine, and saved me from the law of sin and death.'

By a coincidence, or God's Grace, his brother Charles experienced something similar at roughly the same time.

These experiences released an outpouring of energy as these men, proceeded to bring 'saving faith' and 'the assurance of forgiveness' to people willing to believe in Christ and repent of their sins, throughout the country.

They quickly converted talented speakers and charismatic preachers to help them in their work. They brought their converts together to listen to the preachers, and to pray with them, to study the Bible with the teachers, and sing the stirring, melodious hymns written by Charles Wesley. They became members of a Methodist Society, within the Anglican Church. They formed the societies into circuits, and eventually built chapels, which they ran themselves.

They were helped by fellow evangelicals, and hindered and scorned by many who disliked the emotion, the excitement and the sheer energy the new societies engendered.

John Wesley died in 1791, having wished his Methodist Society to remain part of the Established Church. There were many in the Society who desired the opposite. Eventually the Methodists did become an independent denomination, but before that happened Alexander Kilham, a minister on the Sheffield Circuit, broke away from the main body of Methodists. With him was William Thom. Together they formed the Methodist New Connextion in 1797.

During the first half of the 19th century there were further schisms. some major ones, others less so. Hugh Bourne inspired by American open air camp meetings, which involved large numbers of people, held such a meeting at Mow Cop, in Staffordshire. William Clowes was one of the speakers there. They planned more, and were subsequently expelled from the Wesleyan Methodists. Together they founded Primitive Methodism in 1811. This was the most successful of the breakaway groups, and appealed to farm labourers and poor industrial workers especially.

The Independent Methodists seceded in 1817, and remained independent. A dispute over the purchase of an organ for the Brunswick Chapel in Leeds prompted the Protestant Methodists to leave the main body of Methodists in 1827. Later they joined with the Association Methodists, who had formed after their leader, a Dr. Warren of the Bradford Society, was expelled from the Wesleyan Society in 1835.

The Church of the Wesleyan Reformers was established, after a long running campaign against the President of the Wesleyan Conference, Jabez Bunting, in 1849. The man behind this was a James Everett, a minister described as able, eloquent and restless, having a 'mordant wit' and a 'pungent pen'. They had moderate success and were based in Sheffield.

Despite these problems, the Wesleyan Methodists, as they came to be known, made enormous headway. At Wesley's death there had been about seventy-two thousand members of the society, with four times that number of hearers attending the services. By 1820 they had almost two hundred thousand members, but that year showed a decline in numbers for the first time. This was discussed at Conference and the outcome was a belief that it was due to a lack of evangelism. Among a number of resolutions which were passed to prevent a further reduction in numbers was,

> 'Let us endeavour, in our public ministry, to preach constantly all those leading and vital doctrines of the Gospel, which peculiarly distinguished the original Methodist preachers, whose labours were so signally blessed by the Lord, and to preach them in our primitive method – evangelically, experimentally, zealously, and with great plainness and simplicity…. and labouring to apply them closely, affectionately, and energetically to the conscience of the different class of our hearers.'

These resolutions appear to have worked. For the next thirty years, despite breakaway groups, and helped by increasing population, the membership continued to grow. Local circuits initiated revivals in their own areas on a regular basis, which underpinned the strength of the local chapels.

The 1851 religious census shows us how successful the Methodists had become in Yorkshire. In the West Riding alone there were far more chapels than in any other single county in England. Even in the city of York, never at the forefront of protestant nonconformity, there were eight chapels.

1851 Census of Religious Worship Number of Churches

Denomination	East Riding	North Riding	West Riding	Total
Wesleyans	223	304	646	1,173
New Connex.	3		70	73
Prim. Meth	134	110	231	675
Wesley Reform.	1	5	69	75
Wesley Meth. Ass.	1	6	44	51
The total number of Methodist churches in Yorkshire				2,047

There had been no serious alternative to the Anglican Church in the East Riding. Consequently it was fertile ground for the Methodist preachers. Except in the villages wholly owned by an antagonistic squire, they made excellent headway from about 1760. We are told they,

'preached the gospel, with rude and homely eloquence, in barns and sheds and in the open air, and multitudes bowed their souls to God and were converted.'

There is little evidence of evangelical vicars in the East Riding, but there was one. When Methodism was first brought to Langtoft the people were so poor that they could scarcely afford the preacher a night's accommodation. On every visit however, an unknown hand used to place a loaf of bread, a quantity of hay and a small bag of corn at the back door of the house where he stayed. Eventually it was discovered that the local vicar, the Rev. Thomas Atkinson was responsible for this kindness. A common saying of his was,

'If God has a people on earth, the Methodists are among them.'

With or without help, the Methodists made such inroads into the area that by 1851, within the two hundred and twenty parishes of the East Riding, (not every village was a parish), there were two hundred and twenty Wesleyan

Chapels. But they had had a hundred years to accomplish this, and they had become respectable, almost conservative in outlook. As early as 1797 Joseph Entwhistle had complained that Methodism was different from what it had been fifty years earlier. Pew rents had been introduced to clear chapel debts, and the church, now a numerous and respectable body, showed all the signs of stratification and deference to the wealthy trustee.

The story of Primitive Methodism in the East Riding is striking. The Nottingham circuit sent William Clowes to Hull in 1819 where society after society was formed and hundreds were converted. By the end of the century, in Hull alone, there were five circuits with fourteen chapels and ten thousand hearers, a testimony to the strong foundation there.

Two years later he went to mission Scarborough. As he travelled there he preached at Beverley, Driffield, Bridlington, Speeton, Thwing, Fordon and Hunmanby. On January 24th he preached at Flixton, where the, 'whole village was moved.'

Filey had long been noted for its 'wickedness of every description'. Primitive Methodists from Bridlington had tried repeatedly to establish a group there, but had been 'shouted, mobbed and pelted out of the place.'

Johnny Oxtoby took Filey on. He had been born at Great Givendale in 1762, was an agricultural labourer, and spent thirty-seven years 'in sin'. When he became a Wesleyan he obtained peace and proceeded to 'save' his fellow villagers. In 1818 he met William Clowes in Hull, and soon after left the Wesleyans to join the Primitive Methodists, because, he said, 'they had a stronger faith, a warmer ardour, and were more abundant in labours.'

The Sunday he set out for Filey he met a man who knew him. He asked him where he was going. On being told Filey, to save the people, he replied,

'It's a forlorn hope, you had better go back.'

Oxtoby, known all over the Riding as 'praying Johnny' was not deterred. He entered the fishing village and sang along the streets to the beach, where he preached to a rough and rude audience. Eventually he made an impression,

'hearts softened, tears began to flow, and numbers were convinced of the wickedness of their lives.'

As the century progressed, the rivalry between the two branches of Methodism was mainly expressed in chapel building. That apart they often worked together. Joseph Smith, a Huggate yeoman farmer and Wesleyan lay preacher wrote of this in the 1870's. The Wesleyans required a new harmonium, and in order to raise money, Mr Smith agreed to give a lecture on Oliver Cromwell. The Wesleyan chapel was too small, so the Primitives allowed him to use their much larger chapel.

To emphasize the success of the Primitive Methodists, we have a record of a conversation on the train journey between Scarborough and Hull, in the last decade of the 19th century. A Primitive Methodist refuted the allegation that Primitive Methodism was rapidly declining.

He began by saying that when he first had business in Scarborough there was one Primitive chapel, now there were four. As the train moved south he remarked that Filey chapel used to hold five hundred people, now it held nine hundred. The other week at a service there, he was told a third of the adult population was present. At Bridlington and Bridlington Quay there had been two small chapels, each seating about two hundred people, now there were two more, which each held between six and seven hundred people.

At Driffield he could remember the chapel there being twice enlarged, but a year ago one holding one thousand one hundred people had been built. He had visited a small stuffy chapel at Beverley but now noted a new one held eight hundred people. Finally he pointed out Cottingham, a recently built structure twice the size of its predecessor, and that Hull which used to have three small chapels now had twelve.

John Wesley visited most of the larger market towns in the North Riding, and left behind groups of motivated men and women who established societies which became the centre of circuits responsible for taking the Methodist beliefs forward within that extensive area.

The Riding was not well populated and Old Dissent was fairly well established so progress was often slow, but many people who did not commit to membership, still attended as hearers.

Yarm was an early success for the Methodists and its circuit in 1768 extended as far north as Hartlepool in Co. Durham, west as far as Whitby and Robin Hoods Bay, east to Darlington and Northallerton, and south a few miles beyond Thirsk. It included many small communities and such towns as Guisborough, Osmotherley and Stokesley. Scarborough and Easingwold also had extensive circuits.

So successful were these early preachers that by the 19th century the larger towns were heads of their own circuits Whitby was formed in 1783 and by 1816 had seven hundred and twenty-eight members

The Whitby circuit plan for 1835, May to October, shows that thirty-three preachers plus three preachers on trial were employed in the area. To give an example of a preacher's commitment in that six months, they visited the following places, sometimes twice; Glaisdale and Fryup, Goathland, Briggswath, Robin Hoods Bay, [Fyling]Thorpe, Lythe and Sandsend, Ruswarp,

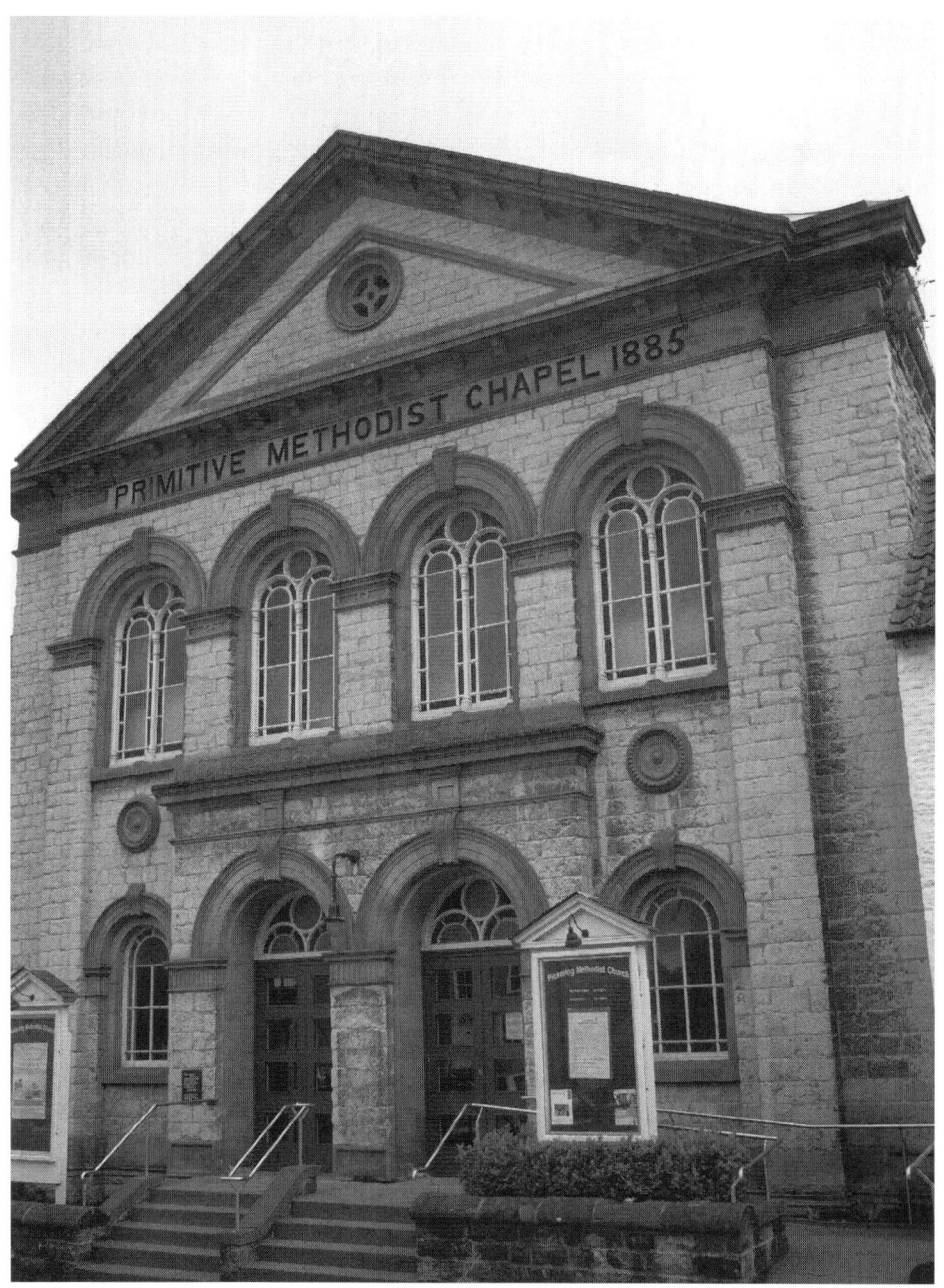

23 Pickering's Primitive Methodist Chapel was built in 1885

Whitby Brunswick, Goldsborough, Newholme and Hutton Mulgrave and Hawsker. The travelling would have been fine in summer, and heroic in winter.

The membership of the circuit in 1841 had risen to one thousand, one hundred and fourteen. Thereafter there was no further increase. The moorland township of Danby formed its own circuit in 1863, with three hundred and thirty-five members, but this dropped to three hundred and four by 1884. Whitby minus the Danby membership had seven hundred and seventy-six members in 1863. This dropped to seven hundred and fifteen, possibly with the advent of the Primitive Methodists. Nevertheless they felt they were doing well enough to demolish two small chapels, and build a much larger one in 1890, because of the increasing number of summer visitors.

Further south the early Scarborough circuit contained villages along the Vale of Pickering, on both sides of the river Derwent, and the towns of Pickering and Malton. By the early 19th century both those towns had their own circuits and worked to establish chapels in communities where there was a sufficiently large membership

In the north west of the Riding, Richmond was the head of a circuit and by 1811 it was said there were about three hundred Methodists in the town. Four years later, the circuit which covered all of Swaledale had a membership of nine hundred and seventy.

A revival in the Reeth area in the 1820's was highly successful. An itinerant preacher wrote about it in the February 1822 Methodist Magazine. He described crowds of lead miners 'pouring down the craggy hills' to worship. The Reeth membership rose from five hundred and twenty to over a thousand under the influence of the evangelical revivalists.

During the 1830's there was a depression in lead mining and the Methodists lost members at this period. By 1851 they had recovered somewhat as the figures for census Sunday show. Richmond had an estimated attendance of three hundred and ninety-four, Reeth had two hundred and forty-one and further west still Gunnerside had three hundred and forty-six. The whole Reeth circuit saw an attendance of one thousand, four hundred adults.

In the Vale of York, Methodist success was probably due to preachers from the Easingwold circuit, but Huntington was so near to York, it seems likely that it would have been within its area of influence. A study of that parish shows how Wesleyan fortunes fluctuated throughout the century.

Poorly served by the Anglican Church there was a group of Methodists by 1786, but twelve years were to pass before they had any premises to meet in. A shoemaker, who moved into the village, opened his house to them. They had a membership of thirty-five people. When this man left the village in 1805, he left them without premises or a leader.

24 William Clowes 1780 – 1851

Two years later, the newly converted, shoemaker's former apprentice, made his house available to the group. By 1809 the membership had fallen to eight. The decline was reversed when two young preachers evangelised the village in 1825. The subsequent surge in membership preceded the building of a chapel, though the members were poor and it became a financial burden on them.

During the 1860's they increased their membership further and the plain rectangular chapel gained a schoolroom, a vestry and a porch, and increased the seating to one hundred and eighty.

A pinnacle of sixty-seven members was reached in 1889 due to outstanding preaching and good leadership. At this period attempts were made to establish a class in West Huntington which failed. There is no mention of Primitive Methodists, clearly where the Wesleyans were struggling, the Primitives may have found it too difficult to gain a foothold.

They did make an impact in other parts of the North Riding, but never as great as in the East Riding. William Clowes came north and visited Scarborough just after Christmas on 27th December 1821, where he preached in the evening and twice the following day, at least once on the beach to a crowd of three thousand. One hundred people were converted and became members and a society was formed. A similar result came from a visit to Whitby a fortnight later.

On the 26th February he preached in a crowded barn in Ayton, where,

'Persecutors raged, but Mr C's mighty prayers calmed them.'

A society of twenty members was formed. The following day he was at neighbouring Seamer 'when many cried for mercy' and five joined the society.

During that year nine men and three women continued Clowes work from the Scarborough society, missioning the local villages. Music was a great help to the Methodists of all kinds, and a note in the newly formed Scarborough society's minutes gives a glimpse of what was involved,

'The singers shall pay for their sittings' and 'Bro B. shall play his clarionet in the singers' pew.' (No doubt the violinist would be relieved to know that) '4s. shall be allowed for repairs to the bass fiddle.'

A promising start was made further north at Guisborough the following year but it did not last. When the town was evangelised again in 1847, this time by some Primitive Methodists from Co. Durham, the result was more enduring. Two years later it was recorded that,

'At this place [Guisborough] things wear a pleasing aspect. The congregations are large and increasing.'

The members took services in all the surrounding ironstone mining communities such as Hutton, Kildale, Brotton, Skelton and Upsall. Primitive Methodists were more politically active than the Wesleyans, and some from Guisborough were active in the Cleveland Miners Association.

While Clowes was in the area he gave the people of Cleveland their first taste of a camp meeting at Moorsome, and missioned Danby and Fryup. The Fryup schoolmaster visited one of the Primitive Methodist meetings and was appalled by the 'hysteria' and the familiar ways in which members of the congregation addressed God.

They persisted and remained a presence in the area, but never a large one. On census Sunday there was only one return made for them and that was at the small hamlet of Houlsyke, where forty people met in a cottage. The following year a small neat chapel was opened there. By the end of the century they had opened chapels at Fryup, Castleton and Danby End.

On the south side of the moors along the Vale of Pickering, they did better, but never approached the strength of the Wesleyans.

Mrs. E Scoby of Cawthorn was a member of a group at Cropton. She wrote the following in a letter to her sister in Farndale in September 1834,

'I do not oft go to Love Feasts but I went to Pickering last Sunday. But this is my sorrow, neither my husband nor sons would go with me. They see no good in them or class meetings....It is the souls of my husband and sons I am concerned for.'

She went on to discuss the Primitive Methodists in the area,

'I hear a good account from Farndale Head. Mr. Fowler is delighted with them and in other places where he has revivals. But we are in a very low way at Cropton, and I thought them very backward at speaking at Pickering. Mr. Fowler spoke well. To do good and to please God is all his desire and I wish to do so too.'

The western Dales were missioned from Brompton near Northallerton which had Primitive Methodists from about 1819, and from where a circuit of travelling preachers was organised.

By 1824 preaching was heard fortnightly at Richmond and Reeth and once every four weeks in Healaugh and Booze in Arkengarthdale. It made little impact at Healaugh, but the others continued and in 1826 a chapel was built in Richmond. The following year the society had twenty-two members. Small classes were held at Hudswell, Booze and Marrick, and at that time there was a total membership including Richmond of about seventy. Though a smaller group than the Wesleyans, they survived. During the depression of the 1830's they only had visiting preachers once a month. The circuit report for 1832 states,

'Reeth has given up entirely and Richmond is not much better.'

They recovered in the following two decades. The religious census returned two Primitive Methodist chapels at Richmond with an average attendance for the previous year of fifty. They survived the century, and became as respected as the Wesleyans but not nearly so successful.

York in the middle of the county had seen Methodists, indeed had had visits from John Wesley in the 18th century. In 1823,

'The Methodists are so numerous a body in York as to render two regular places of worship.....necessary for their accommodation.' The principal chapel was in New St., and held two thousand people. The other chapel in Albion St., was about half the size. As demand increased, by 1826 they had built a third chapel in Walmgate.

By this time the Primitive Methodists were also in the area. William Clowes made York a target in 1819 when he preached 'on the Pavement'. When he finished he gave out his name and said he would return in a fortnight.

When he next preached at York thousands listened, a room was taken and a society formed. But this success did not last and preachers were soon being harassed. An extract from the journal of a Mr. Hutchinson tells us,

'Sunday March 4 1821. I preached in the evening at York to a numerous and attentive congregation, supposed to consist of 1,200. We had more peace this evening than ever before. Perhaps this was due to the extraordinary and Christian like conduct of Lord Dundas, the present Lord Mayor of York. His Lordship attended the service having heard how we were molested, and determined we should have the peace and quiet which the laws of the country allow.'

By 1823 they had taken over a former small Calvinist chapel in Grape Lane. They were still there in 1840, but by the end of the century they had four chapels and a mission room.

The poor people living in the industrial areas of the West Riding were fertile ground for the Methodists, although when the Wesleys first began to preach in Yorkshire towns they often faced hostility. Charles Wesley wrote 'Hell from beneath was moved to oppose us', when he first visited Sheffield.

Once they had established a society in those towns they moved quickly across the Riding, and the industrial areas responded. The original Wesleyan Methodists remained the largest group, but there was strong support for the breakaway groups such as the New Connexion, and the Wesleyan Reformers, who appealed to the industrial poor. The Primitive Methodists especially did very well, attracting and retaining the loyalty of farm labourers and mining communities.

On census Sunday in Leeds there were good attendances at seven Wesleyan chapels, also at the four Primitive Methodist, three Wesleyan Methodist Association, one New Connexion and one Wesleyan Protestant Methodist chapel.

In south Yorkshire, dominated by Sheffield, Rotherham, Barnsley and Doncaster, iron, steel and coal were the major industries, but towards the west and the east, and sometimes alongside, were rural villages. In 1851 this area recorded one hundred and thirty-one Wesleyan chapels with twenty five regular meetings in private houses where there was no chapel. These people recorded twenty-nine point five percent of the total attendances at religious services. The Primitive Methodists were the next largest group with forty-seven congregations, and the Wesleyan Reformers, had nineteen. The Methodist New Connexion, which had flourished in the Sheffield area since it was formed, was also well represented.

These societies had been established and sustained by people such as Thomas Naylor, known as 'The Father of Methodism' in Doncaster who died three years later. His obituary in the Doncaster Gazette said,

> 'He knew Methodism in its most unpopular form, He stood side by side with a minister from Sheffield when the voice of the multitude assailed them with scorn and derision…. He was everywhere welcomed as a faithful exponent of the Gospel.'

At the opposite end of the Riding in the Dales, there had been a sprinkling of Methodists from the late 18th century, but because the communities were small and scattered it would appear where societies were formed and chapels built, they were mainly Wesleyan. As in the North Riding Dales the Primitive Methodists only had a limited impact, with chapels in a few of the larger market towns such as Ripon, Pateley Bridge and Settle.

An elderly Daleswoman wrote of her experiences at the end of the 19th century in 'The Dalesman',

25 Talbot Lane Methodist Chapel Rotherham West Riding. Built at the very end of the century on the site of the original chapel visited by John Wesley

'The chapel has exerted a strong influence in local life, and Methodists in the Dales, meeting in small communities play a notable part in social affairs. They have plain buildings, but they are plain folk with plain ways. Their faith is simple but strong.'

Yorkshire was one of the English counties where small communities of Roman Catholics survived after the Reformation. They endured the punitive periods of the 17th and to a lesser extent the 18th centuries.

There had always been a number in the larger towns where they lived inconspicuously and were for the most part left alone. There were more cohesive communities living around and protected by wealthy Catholic aristocrats and gentry. These became fewer throughout the 18th century, and resulted in the dispersal of some of these rural Catholics usually into the increasingly populous industrial areas of the county.

Having been perceived as a national threat for so long, head counts were often taken, and while perhaps not completely accurate and possibly incomplete, they are an indication of how many Catholics were living in the county. A return made in 1787 gave five hundred and fifty-nine people in the East Riding, one thousand, eight hundred and eighty-one people in the West Riding, and two thousand, three hundred and seventy-two people in the North Riding. This total of four thousand, four hundred and thirty-five Catholics in Yorkshire as a whole was just over one percent of the entire Yorkshire population.

They were served by twenty-eight secular priests, twenty-five Jesuits, and twenty monastic personnel. Since priests often served more than one mass house, it seems likely that there were at least one hundred of these at the beginning of the 19th century, although most of these would have been small single rooms, often within a larger building. There were a few actual chapels, in places such as York, or gentry houses such as Hazlewood Castle near Tadcaster.

Three factors affected the growth in numbers throughout the 19th century. At the very end of the 18th century, the attitude of the British government towards Catholics was affected by the persecution of Catholic priests in France during the French Revolution. Some of these priests fled to England, where they were made welcome, and some settled for a number of years.

Legislation known as the Catholic Relief Acts, passed in 1829 followed this growing acceptance of Catholics, gave them the confidence to build more chapels and start to evangelise the local people.

The greatest impact was made by increasing numbers of Irish immigrants who came to England mostly after the Potato Famine in 1845. They could be found in the countryside, sometimes on a seasonal basis, but settled mostly in the industrial areas.

In the East Riding the Constable family of Everingham remained loyal Catholics into the 19th century. We know there was a mass house there in 1764, when the parish had about twenty-five Catholic families. By 1822 a Catholic chapel had been built in the nearby market town of Pocklington, seventeen years later another one was built within Everingham parish itself.

There were ten recorded Catholic chapels in the East Riding by 1851, to serve an estimated three thousand people, but these remained roughly within the same areas as before, that is the area to the north and east of Hull, and areas to the south and east of Pocklington.

Hull itself, once a strongly protestant if not puritan town had only fifteen Catholics in 1796, but a French émigré priest, Abbe Foucher came to minister to them and when he returned to France in 1820 he said that he 'left behind to his successor a numerous congregation and a fine establishment'. This was well before the Irish immigrants arrived and so it appears Yorkshire people were being converted.

The Hull Catholics continued to prosper and multiply. In 1826 they purchased a piece of ground on Jarratt street on which they built a larger church, dedicated to St. Charles. When it was opened in July 1829 there were twelve priests attending. The building was extended in the following years.

For Catholics living on the east side of the river Hull the school-chapel of St. Mary was opened in 1856, and by the 1890's had a large new church building. The following year the convent of the Sisters of Mercy was founded on Anlaby Rd., and within eighteen years opened a school for six hundred girls and infants, plus forty select pupils. A boys' school had been opened in 1863. Hull Catholics did well in the 19th century.

The north of the riding had few Catholics through most of the century. Following the conversion of Lady Jessica, wife of Sir Tatton Sykes of Sledmere, a mission hall was opened in Driffield in 1883. Three years later a church dedicated to Our Lady and St. Edward replaced it, providing spiritual comfort for the many seasonal Irish labourers who came to the Wolds farms. Lady Jessica, no doubt a visitor to the resort of Bridlington, may well have influenced the decision to build a Catholic church there in 1886.

A more unusual establishment was the Yorkshire Catholic Reformatory for Boys, built at Holme on Spalding Moor by Sir Edward Vavasour of Hazlewood Castle in the West Riding. It had accommodation for two hundred and twenty-two boys, and we are told, 'The institution is always well filled.'

North Riding Catholics were also dependent on wealthy landowning Catholics to protect them and provide a mass house and priest. About two thousand, five hundred Catholics lived in scattered communities across the Riding, with larger concentrations in Cleveland and the Whitby area, western Ryedale and Richmondshire.

The first half of the century saw a modest increase in numbers in the North Riding, but when equated with the general growth in population it was unremarkable.

Exiled French priests obtained property at Ampleforth in Ryedale, where they established the St. Lawrence Catholic College in 1802. They were also active in Whitby and district, and were possibly influential in providing new premises for worship in Scarborough in 1803.

A French priest served the Catholics in Richmond where a new chapel was built in 1811 and enlarged in 1855. As in Hull the missionary zeal of the exiles was rewarded.

Some small communities with no rich patron were less successful. The market town of Stokesley in Cleveland can serve as an example of many similar places where Catholics struggled. It had had a Mass House in 1745, which was burnt down by a mob during the Jacobite Rebellion. This was not rebuilt. At the start of the 19th century the number of Catholics had decreased to about twenty, although there were a few in the surrounding villages.

There were Franciscans at Osmotherley about twelve miles to the south, and they probably served the Stokesley Catholics who remained without a resident priest until 1861.

The Catholic chapel which was established in Stokesley in 1861 was a converted granary loft above the stables in the yard of the Angel Inn. This was the Mass house that the Catholic Bishop of Beverley, (who was in charge of all Yorkshire Catholics at that time,) inspected in 1865, and where he decided that it was, 'sufficiently large for present wants.' He did however give the priest a cheque to widen the alter and make other cosmetic improvements.

While he was at Stokesley he confirmed thirteen boys and four girls. The total number of Catholics in the area in that year was given as one hundred at Stokesley, sixty at Osmotherley and six at Crathorne. Numbers continued to increase and it became apparent a church was required.

The Bishop of Beverley was offered a donation of a £1,000 to build a church at Castleford in the West Riding. The donor was persuaded that Stokesley had the greater need, since the industrial area surrounding Castleford was more capable than Stokesley of raising the finance for a new building.

The church of St Joseph was opened in 1873 before a large congregation. Priests from Egton Bridge and Ugthorpe, long established Catholic communities, were among the nine priests who officiated at the opening service and consecration.

In 1801 the population of Middlesbrough had been twenty-five people. Between 1831 and 1841 it was developed as a new industrial town and port. The industry was based on iron foundries using ore mined in Cleveland and Rosedale on the North Yorkshire Moors. By 1851 the population was seven thousand, six hundred and thirty-one, and it continued to grow. By 1901 the number of people in the new town had risen to ninety-one thousand, three hundred and three, almost as many as Hull.

There were three thousand, six hundred and twenty-two Irish immigrants entered on the Middlesbrough Census return for 1871. Such a large influx of Catholics probably resulted in the creation of the Catholic Diocese of Middlesbrough seven years later. This replaced the Diocese of Beverley, and covered the North and East Ridings, along with the York parishes on the northern bank of the Ouse.

The West Riding and the remaining York parishes were administered by a new Diocese of Leeds. The reorganisation acknowledged the increasing number of Catholics in the industrial areas and a much slighter but significant increase in the rural areas. These Catholic communities continued to grow to the end of the century and the population continued to increase, as did immigration both from Ireland and the other two more rural Ridings.

At the end of the 18th century the population of the West Riding had not had a high percentage of Catholics, and those could only be found in about thirty percent of West Riding parishes. Some places may only have had one family, some like Spofforth had over forty families. Most had a few.

Unless connected to a wealthy family like the Vavasours of Hazlewood Castle, or the Gascoines of Lotherton Hall, they usually worshipped in small premises, led by itinerant priests, until the Catholic Relief Acts gave them the confidence to build churches, and this only happened when the money was available. Increasingly rural Catholics were moving out of the countryside, and so the majority of Catholic churches were built in urban areas.

In Wakefield one was built by 1828 and three years later there was one at Knaresborough, which could also serve the nearby Spa of Harrogate. Doncaster had a Catholic church by 1833. In 1858 it was reported that,

> 'In the summertime the chapel is filled to overflowing, and vast numbers of Irish reapers are obliged to be content with the accommodation afforded by the open space near the building.'

The Duke of Norfolk, England's premier Catholic magnate owned most of the land in Sheffield. About two hundred and fifty Catholics heard mass in the Duke's house there in the early 19th century. This was sufficiently convenient, that the Duke did not build his imposing church of St. Marie's in Norfolk Row, until 1847. In 1851 the congregation there was given as about two thousand people at morning mass. There was also a small chapel in Victoria St., where two hundred and fifty more people attended mass.

This steady growth of Catholicism in Yorkshire was, for the most part accepted by the protestant communities. York where there had been two churches since the 18th century, plus a convent and school, had a Catholic mayor in the 1830's. More surprising was a Catholic mayor of Leeds during the same period.

In 1839, Cardinal Houseman, describing a visit to Huddersfield, said that Catholics,

26 An Irish immigrant family. Family size was initially large amongst Irish immigrants

'can do what they please, bigotry is at an end, and processions may walk the streets with no more fear of molestation than in Rome.'

This was a little premature. The restoration of a hierarchy, which created a Bishop of Beverley in 1850, set toleration back for a time.

The Leeds Mercury referred to it as, 'Papal insult to England.' While the Yorkshire Gazette, 'urged all protestants to be alert to fight this ecclesiastical tyranny.' Such headlines were followed by attacks on churches, priests and nuns. Once more the Catholics had to keep a low profile.

Many of these people were of Irish descent. In 1851, eight point nine percent of the population of Bradford, (nine thousand, two hundred and seventy-nine people), were born in Ireland, and a further four point nine percent of the population of Leeds, (eight thousand, four hundred and sixty-six people).

This immigration continued after the potato famine and peaked in 1871, by which time there were fifty-eight thousand, one hundred and seventy-one people living in Yorkshire who had been born in Ireland.

The majority moved around, but some settled and small Catholic communities were formed within the wider industrial population.

Such a community was established just outside Rotherham where there had never been many Catholics since the Reformation. At Masbrough, St.

Bede's church was built in 1843 to serve the people working in the iron foundries there. It was restored and extended in 1873.

Jesuits worked for short periods at Broughton Hall and Wakefield. An exception was Richard Sharp, a Jesuit who lived and worked at Skipton from 1874 to 1914. As a member of the Board of Guardians he defended the rights of poor Catholics and was one of the promoters of the Skipton and District Hospital. When he died he was described as one of 'the landmarks of the town'.

Though the English Catholic gentry still played their part in supporting their religion, by 1901, forty-eight thousand, nine hundred and seventeen people living in Yorkshire, had been born in Ireland. In addition, there were thousands of Irish immigrants who had died since they arrived in Yorkshire, but were the parents of Catholics. The result was a large increase in Catholic churches, missions and schools. It saw a change in the origins of the people who worked in these institutions, priests, monks and nuns, from English upper and middle class to a mixture of English, Irish and continental religious.

There was a small synagogue in Hull at the end of the 18th century. A watchmaker called Michael Levy was possibly the leader of the community which numbered between twenty and thirty people in 1796.

Hull was the port of entry for Jewish immigrants fleeing persecution in Russia during the latter half of the 19th century. This no doubt increased the Jewish population in Hull, which was already slightly bigger in 1851, where the synagogue saw an attendance of 74 in the morning, 17 in the afternoon and 21 in the evening. Seven years later a burial ground was acquired, and by the end of the century a second synagogue had been built.

Some of the Jews who came through Hull made their way to Middlesbrough. They had a synagogue there in the 1870's

There were a few German Jewish woollen traders in Bradford from the end of the 18th century. They lived in an area known as 'Little Germany'. In nearby Leeds, the 1841 census of population tells us that there were nine families and a few single individuals making a total of fifty-six people. The Earl of Cardigan had granted them a piece of land for a burial ground in 1837, and a synagogue existed by 1846, but the numbers increased slowly. In 1861 there were still only about two hundred.

The vast majority of later immigrants made for Leeds. The Lancet towards the end of the century commented,

'During the last 20 years a steady influx of Polish Russian Jews, ... on starting are often acquainted with but one word of English, and that is Leeds.'

70

It went on to say that there was between 1,200 and 1,400 men plus about 500 Jewesses, working in the tailoring profession there.

The only other industrial town of any size with a Jewish community was Sheffield, but this was not the magnet Leeds was, and by the end of the century there were only about six hundred living there.

Wherever there was a charismatic person, with or without a desire to found their own group; or a disagreement with the rules or people governing an existing church, there was a strong chance a new group would become established. Sometimes they stayed within a locality, sometimes they had a wider appeal.

Such a group which lingered on from the 18th century was the 'Southcottians'. These were the followers of Johanna Southcott, the daughter of a Devon farmer, born in 1750, and self-styled prophetess. In 1792 she revealed she was the woman who in the Book of Revelations, would give birth to the new Messiah, plus other dubious forecasts. She is believed to have had over one hundred thousand followers at the time of her death in 1814.

Some of these were in Leeds, in 1837,

'A few of the deluded 'Southcottians' still remain and assemble in a room in George St.' There were also a number in Sheffield where they assembled in the Free Masons Hall, in Paradise Square.'

They were still in the West Riding over twenty years later. On the 14th December 1863, it was reported in the press that,

'At the Wakefield Court House, an American named Daniel Milton, who is connected with the Southcottian Sect, was fined for a trespass upon the property of the executors of John Wroe, deceased, at Wrenthorpe, the prophet of the society.'

People with unconventional religious ideas, coming from across the Atlantic can also be evidenced in the advent of the Spiritualists. The first Spiritualist Church in England was established in Keighley in 1853.

The Mormons had adherents in England by 1837. They appear on the religious census of 1851, the estimated number in England and Wales being thirty-four thousand, one hundred and eighty-two. For Sheffield the entry tells us that the Church of Jesus Christ of Latter Day Saints had a congregation of forty-six. They met in what had 'lately been a dwelling house.'

They were more numerous in Leeds where there was a church which could seat two hundred and forty. The attendance was one hundred in the morning, one hundred and fifty in the afternoon and two hundred in the evening. There is no evidence for them in Hull, even at the end of the century.

The Christian Brethren were more successful. They were a splinter group from the Methodist New Connection, and were led by Joseph Barker of Newcastle. They had a small congregation in Arkengarthdale in the middle of the century, with 16 worshippers on Census Sunday. The chapel was not used after about 1865. They appear to be established in Scarborough by 1881 where they met in a room in Swan Hill Rd., The estimated attendance was one hundred and thirty-nine

Leeds had two places of worship for 'Brethren' and one of those may have been for Christian Brethren. There were also Plymouth and Exclusive Brethren by this time. 'Brethren' are also mentioned in a few other more populous places later in the century but it is unclear which particular 'Brethren' they are.

The Swedenborgians, whose centre was in Lancashire had a church in Bradford plus one or two others in the West Riding during the century. They followed the teachings of Emmanuel Swedenborg, a Swedish scientist and diplomat who taught, 'there are correspondences between the visible forms of nature and the invisible world of the spirit'.

27 William Booth 1829 – 1912

The most successful of the new denominations of the 19th century was the Salvation Army. It was founded in 1865 by William Booth and his wife. He was a former Methodist minister who modelled his organisation on the army. Its members were 'officers' and 'soldiers'. They wore a uniform, used bands and banners, the church was called a citadel, and its publication was the 'War Cry'.

An evangelical religious community, it was reminiscent of the early Methodists. It had highly emotional open air services, where it was so much easier to join a crowd, than enter a church, and where good tunes were played by a brass band

Another former primitive Methodist, Captain Elijah Cadman arrived in Whitby in 1877 he handed out bills which read,

'War! War! In Whitby, 2,000 men and women wanted at once to join the Salvation Army, that is making an attack on the Devil's Kingdom.'

In time Cadman became a Major with the Yorkshire Division, where he had huge success opening corps at York, Scarborough, Halifax and Shipley.

Yorkshire had always responded well to this type of Christianity and continued to do so. Sheffield had a branch by 1879, which prospered and by 1894 they had a citadel on one of the main streets in the city centre.

General Booth visited Scarborough in 1881 where he was involved in plans to build the first Citadel. The success of the 'Salvationists' in Scarborough was amazing. On Sunday 4th December in the same year, they held six services in Scarborough; at St. George's Hall, and The Circus. The attendances, which were specifically counted by the staff of the Scarborough Mercury were; seven hundred and twenty in the morning, two thousand, six hundred and sixty in the afternoon, and three thousand, three hundred and eighty in the evening. These numbers were swelled further by people (not counted) who attended after other church services were over.

By the early 1890's, the Salvation Army in Hull had seven places of worship, which included the East Riding Divisional Headquarters. In total they could accommodate about five thousand people.

If the number of Places of Worship that were built, rebuilt and/or extended during the 19th century were a measure of the religious devotion of the population, then that devotion in Yorkshire was deep and extensive.

This devotion sprang, primarily, but not entirely from the Evangelical Revival. All parts of Yorkshire were affected, but particularly the rural East Riding where Methodism, Wesleyan and Primitive, had chapels in almost every parish, and the industrial areas where not only Methodists, but to a lesser degree evangelical Anglicans, Independents and Baptists made converts and sustained larger congregations.

Through the century, as the population grew ever larger, these people had revivals, and continued to mission new areas as well as established congregations, with spectacular success. A major factor in this continued success was the qualities of the ministers. A mesmerising and charismatic preacher could unite and enthuse a congregation. A dull and uninspiring one would soon see empty pews.

This applied equally to Anglican clerics, especially those whose High Church views sometimes offended people unused to vestments and ornament in their church.

Such matters did not affect the enormous growth, primarily through immigration, of the strength and numbers of Roman Catholicism. Free from penal laws, they spread, mainly throughout the Yorkshire towns. Where Catholic churches flourished in the countryside, they were usually those of old established Yorkshire Catholic communities.

Despite the size of congregations at all places of worship showing an increase from the beginning of the century, only about fifty per cent of the population attended a place of worship by the middle of the century. This meant about half the people in the county, as in the country, appear to have had little faith of any kind, except perhaps enduring superstition.

The religious 'census' taken by newspapers in a number of towns, including those in Yorkshire suggest that the percentage of the 'faithless' had reduced very little, if at all by the end of the century. Nevertheless, it is likely that the 19th century saw more genuine active and participating Christianity than had been the case in earlier centuries.

BIBLIOGRAPHY

Primary Sources
West Ayton Library.North Yorkshire.
Reminiscenses of Thomas Hebblethwaite.
Ryedale Folk Museum. Hutton le Hole, North Yorkshire
John Rushton Archive. (19th century correspondence).

Published Sources

D. Allen. St. Joseph's Stokesley. Stockton, 1972.
W. Allott. Leeds Quaker Meeting. Leeds, 1966.
E. Baines (ed.) Baines Yorkshire. North, East and West Ridings.
Wakefield, 1823.
J. Binns. A History of Scarborough North Yorkshire From Earliest Times to the
Year 2000. Pickering, 2001.
G. Bullett. Sydney Smith a Biography and Collection of his Writings.
London, 1959.
T. Bulmer & Co. History, Topography, and Directory of East Yorkshire.
Preston, 1892.
P Chrystal. The Rowntree Family of York, Pickering, 2013.
F.L. Cross (Ed.) The Oxford Dictionary of the Christian Church. London,
1957.
F. Crowder & D. Green. Rotherham. Wakefield, 1971.
R.E. Davies. Methodism. Harmondsworth, 1963.
M. Freedman. 'The Leeds Jewish Community: A Sketch of its History
and Development.' Aspects of Leeds. Ed. L. Stevenson Tate, Barnsley,
1998.
R. Fieldhouse & B. Jennings. A History of Richmond & Swaledale.
Chichester, 1978.
B.J.D. Harrison & G.Dixon (eds.) Guisborough before 1900. Gt. Ayton,
1981.
S. Harrison. The History of Driffield. Pickering, 2002.
D. Hey. 'The Changing Patterns of Nonconformity, 1660-1851. Essays in the
Social and Economic History of South Yorkshire Ed. S Pollard, Sheffield, 1976.
D. Hey. Yorkshire From A.D.1000. London, 1986.
D. Hey. A History of Sheffield. Lancaster, 1998.
J. Marsland. Whitby Methodist Circuit Bicentenary, 1783-1983. Lincoln,

1983.

J. Mayhall. Annals of Yorkshire Vol 2. Leeds.

D. Neave. Port, Resort and Market Town A History of Bridlington. Hull, 2000.

N. Pevsner & D. Neave. Yorkshire: York and the East Riding, London, 1996.

Post Office. Directory of Yorkshire. 1857.

M. Rowlands. The Quakers of Kirbymoorside and District, 1652-1990. Kirbymoorside, 1990.

A. Rowntree (ed.) The History of Scarborough. London 1931.

D. Rubenstein. Yorkshire Friends in Historical Perspective. York, 2005.

J. Rushton. They Kept Faith. Pickering, 1970.

J. Rushton. The History of Ryedale North Yorkshire. Pickering, 2003

W. Pearson Thistlethwaite. Yorkshire Quarterly Meetings of the Society of Friends 1665-1966. 1979.

I. Sellars (ed.) Our Heritage, The Baptists of Lancashire, Yorkshire and Cheshire 1647-1987. Leeds, 1987.

J.F. Supple-Green. The Catholic Revival in Yorkshire 1850-1900. Leeds, 1990.

H. Woodcock. Sketches of Primitive Methodism on the Wolds. London.

F. Wrigley. The History of the Yorkshire Congregational Union. London, 1923.

CHAPTER 3

RELIGION IN YORKSHIRE IN THE TWENTIETH CENTURY

1900 – 1930

Historical Yorkshire at the beginning of the 20th century had a population of over three and a half million people. They were not spread evenly across the county. The East Riding, had the smallest population, around four hundred thousand. A large proportion of these people lived in the only large town and port of Hull, and the less extensive Beverley and Bridlington. Apart from a few small market towns, everywhere else in the Riding was rural, producing mainly corn and sheep.

The North Riding was by far the largest in area, but again predominantly agricultural. The previous fifty years had seen much development in the new industrial town of Middlesbrough, which was catching up with its rival Hull in size and importance, but the other towns in the riding such as Scarborough, Whitby, Northallerton and Richmond, were not much bigger than the market towns of, Malton, Helmsley, Yarm, Masham and a few others. Because much of the riding was bleak moorland, its population was only about fifty thousand more than its smaller neighbour.

The West Riding, with its own share of sparsely peopled moors, nevertheless contained a population of about three million. They lived mainly in the area bordered by the towns of Bradford, Leeds, Wakefield, Huddersfield and Halifax, where there were collieries, factories and a thriving textile industry. In the south of the Riding, Sheffield, Rotherham, Doncaster and Barnsley also had sizeable populations which serviced the collieries, foundries and steelworks in the area. Around and within these districts there was a considerable amount of agriculture. Some villages were part industrial. Some had no industry at all.

In 1851 the only official census of religion ever taken, showed that approximately half the population of England attended no place of worship at all on census Sunday, and that about half of the people who did attend, went to a Methodist church. There were variations on these figures, but Yorkshire was broadly in line with the rest of the country.

The Yorkshire variations saw the East Riding, overwhelmingly Methodist, with a moderate attendance at the Anglican Church, and just a few Congregationalists, Baptists, Quakers and Catholics. The North Riding also had more Methodists than any other denomination, but less than the East Riding. The Anglican attendance was also less than in the East Riding, but there were considerably more of the other branches of nonconformity, and Catholics. In the West Riding the Methodists again were a considerable majority, but the Established church had less support than the sum of the other groups.

An increasing population, and considerable effort by most Christian churches in Yorkshire, saw congregations increase, and more and larger churches and chapels being built to accommodate them in the following fifty years.

The large congregations that most churches enjoyed by the beginning of the 20th century therefore were not because inroads had been made into the half of the population that did not attend church. From what few statistics there are, it seems more than possible that ground was being lost, albeit slowly, and by no means uniformly.

The Established Church of England, or Anglican Church, had made an enormous effort in the previous century to provide free accommodation for the poorer people of all their parishes, and in creating new parishes in the heavily populated areas. Most parishes had a resident clergyman; a rector, vicar or curate, sometimes a vicar and a curate.

Some of these clergy were poles apart in the type of Christianity they preached and how they preached it. The Evangelicals were similar to the enthusiastic nonconformists, especially the Methodists. The successful ones were charismatic preachers, who cared deeply and worked hard for all their parishioners. They held their simple services in unadorned churches, and were usually well liked, if not loved by their flock. These sincere, pious men were said to be 'Low' Church.

The 'High Church' clergy were also known as Anglo Catholics. They used vestments, ornaments, candles and incense in the Roman Catholic manner. They introduced choirs, confession and Anglican nuns, along with more elaborate services, ideal for churchgoers who liked church as theatre with a touch of mysticism, less so for those who preferred a restrained simple service. The High Church had its inspirational preachers, but in such churches ritual was more important than preaching.

Between these two extremes and rivals, were a large number of Anglican clergymen who belonged to neither. Possibly less spiritual but probably more professional, they were described as belonging to a 'Broad

28 St Margaret's Church in Leeds was completed in 1908. It is now an Arts Centre

Church'. Some of them practised 'muscular Christianity', emphasising a sense of duty, public service, healthy, sporting activity and outdoor pursuits.

All the genuinely parochially minded Anglican clergy, however identified, were heavily involved in many types of social work and education within their spheres of influence, which would help all the people in their parishes. Clarence Walker of Elsecar in the parish of Wentworth in the West Riding, remembered the Rev. Charles Moslesworth Sharpe, vicar for thirty-four years in the early 20th century, in these words,

> '[He] was a bachelor of independent means, ideally suited to his ministry...an Anglican with strong convictions and would not be dissuaded by criticisms. He did much for the poor, food parcels were sent to those in need anonymously.

Further to the east at Denaby near Doncaster, where a colliery had been opened in 1868, Robert Henry Shephard started work at the mine in 1901, when he was fourteen years old. He was a good footballer and recalled that,

> 'in 1905 [I] played with Denaby Church team, in the Mexborough Sunday School League. I played three years with the church team, then .was given a trial with Denaby United. In 1910/11 I was asked if I wanted a transfer to Doncaster Rovers, but I decided to stay at the pit.

We had Bible class on Sunday afternoons with more than a hundred members; the vicar was the Rev. F.S. Hawkes and the curate was the Rev. Kenneth Kirk. I still went to Bible class after I went to play for Denaby United. The vicar and the curate travelled home and away games with us, they gave a lot of enthusiasm and support and were very well respected. It was a sad day when the vicar...and the curate left the Denaby church. They had very good congregations at the church services. I don't think the same has been as popular since.'

A more usual approach to religion in the same area, was told by Harriet Hallett, born in Mexborough in 1902, one of ten children of another Denaby miner. She left school at thirteen, but did some weekend work before that. One woman she worked for was a 'grand old lady' called Mrs. Venables.

'She was a Salvation Army woman, and she was the first person to take me to the seaside, to Cleethorpes with the Salvation Army.'

After she left school, Harriet went to work in Sheffield, living at her aunt's.

'I think I stopped there about four month, well I didn't know anybody and my aunt were a big church woman.'

She went on to say why she left,

'Oh, she were very pious, and that didn't suit me. Well I hadn't been brought up to that. We went to chapel as kids, but I mean, it were too restricted. It weren't like our family anyway, free and easy.'

In the North Riding, the Helmsley vicar was a High churchman with an extremely authoritarian manner. He had a choir and incense in his high decorated church, confession and Anglican nuns. In the large area under his control he was rarely opposed except by Nonconformists in the town, who could afford to be independent. The gentry and all people who considered themselves members of the establishment attended his church. As did the poor, who depended on charity to a large extent, and could not afford to offend the people liable to provide help.

A Primitive Methodist in the East Riding was not too impressed by the new Anglican Clergy. At the turn of the century, he wrote,

'The old easy going parsons have nearly all passed away, and now there are the preaching, praying, pastorating clergy working hard to satisfy the religious wants of the people, and anxious to discredit our ministry.'

He went on to explain the loss of some Methodist members,

'In most of our villages Methodism maintains its ground; in a few it is declining. The descendants of some wealthy Methodists leave the chapel for the church. They are said to prefer a liturgy to simple worship; robed priests and surpliced choirs to men in ordinary garb; short sermons to long ones; clergymen to local preachers; a Gothic church to a plain chapel and association with the rich, to the companionship of shopkeepers and the labouring classes. Hence it is that some children of chapel going parents have passed over to the church.'

In 1901, the Anglican Church reached its peak in numbers of clergy employed, and by implication in attendances at church. There were twenty-five thousand, two hundred and thirty-five clergymen in England in that year, and the numbers have declined ever since. The early 20th century saw the last great effort by the Church of England to recover ground lost to the Nonconformists or more particularly to make inroads into the great number of people of little or no faith. They built a few more churches, often in the spreading suburbs of larger towns, and for the urban poor they opened mission rooms which served for services alongside social work.

The Wesleyans were the parent body of several branches of Methodism, and by far the most numerous. The next largest group, also very successful in Yorkshire, were the Primitive Methodists, particularly so in the East Riding. The Methodist New Connection, The Protestant Methodists and the Wesleyan Reformers originated in the West Riding, and had fairly large memberships in the industrial areas.

Recollections in 'The Dalesman' magazine tell of experiences of Methodism in the Yorkshire Dales at the beginning of the 20th century. Mary Crewe wrote,

'I was brought up in a religious home and from my earliest days attended chapel. Most English homes could be called religious in those days. Grandfather Wood was a Methodist class leader. Before his conversion during a revival, he had been a sidesman in the village

[Anglican] church. The vicar at that time was heavily against Nonconformists.'

Another contributor tells us that in her chapel at that period,

'Those were the days of 'Sermon testers', who would have complained if it had been too short and sweet! It was; firstly, secondly, thirdly, fourthly and finally my brethren; and there was no watering it down for the children. They had to behave themselves or take the consequences.'

Some of the preachers were extremely dramatic, both in their extempore praying, and their sermons. When using the Prodigal Son as a text, one lay preacher would dash to the chapel window,

'Aye. t'lads coming, Sarah,' he would shout, 'Kill t'fatted calf, lass.'

In the old days, there were many revivals. Chapel folk had to go round the village missioning, singing in procession. The young lads used to hold the lanterns and compose lines of their own to the tunes that were being sung. In the south of the county Clarence Walker remembered,

'Several Nonconformist ministers and laymen worked hard for the poor and provided them with many comforts. These laymen worked in the mines devoting their spare time to others, though they were no better off than those they helped, perhaps a little more prudent with their money. The youngsters were encouraged to attend Sunday School … they were taught a good moral code which made many of them realise a better way existed, and they often grew into better citizens than their parents.'

Proud of the way that, after a few years of rivalry, the Wesleyans and the Primitive Methodists had worked well together in the East Riding, where there was at least one chapel in almost every village, a lay preacher wrote,

'For seventy years the Wesleyans and Primitive Methodists have worked side by side, shoulder to shoulder, in dispelling ignorance and saving souls along these Wolds, but with little friction….. A few years ago the two denominations united in holding a mission, now in the Wesleyan, now in the Primitive chapels…..A speaker said "We Wesleyans and Primitives are going to fight the devil side by side with

29 Northallerton Methodist Church

each other. If we villagers can unite in getting the people into our chapels, the towns folk will learn a lesson and they will become united more and more. ('Yes, bless Him, cried a Primitive brother in the Gallery') Why should there not be a Methodist Federation?"

This early evidence of ecumenicalism was when the Methodists were still very strong, not just in the countryside, but in every part of Yorkshire. Amalgamation and pooling resources made sense when numbers were no longer rising, but matters had not yet become so critical that action was taken by the three major Methodist churches.

Though not as numerous as the Methodists and the Anglicans, the Old Dissenting denominations; the Congregationalists and the Baptists were also influential in the early 20th century.

The long established Congregational churches were often economically sound, having an endowment to rely on. Usually found in towns, they held to the Calvinist doctrine of predestination. Heaven was for the elect. and Calvinists were of the elect. All other people, no matter how they lived their lives, would not go to heaven. The members of these churches, which were autonomous, but in loose association with each other, were usually middle class, well to do professional and tradespeople. As early as 1928 they ordained their first female minister, spearheading a movement which increased among all the major denominations except Catholicism in the second half of the century.

The Baptists, who as their name suggests, believe in adult baptism had a few churches in the countryside, but like the Congregationalists were mainly an urban church. Also like the Congregationalists the Particular Baptists were Calvinists, a smaller group, the General Baptists were Arminian in doctrine. Like the Methodists they believed in the saving grace of God for all sinners who repented. Baptist numbers slowly continued to increase in the early years of the 20th century, only starting to decline during the First World War.

Most of the former Presbyterian churches had become Unitarians in the 18th century, when they were also known as 'Rational Dissenters'. They did not believe in the Trinity, and were open to Darwin's theory of evolution, along with other contemporary scientific thought. Like the other Old Dissenting congregations, these were mainly middle class, well educated people whose churches were found in towns. They were a minority church, and remained so, but nevertheless survived as a denomination to the end of the 20th century.

The Society of Friends, more commonly called Quakers were initially quite successful in gaining followers in all parts of the county, in both rural areas and the towns, but started to lose membership through the 18th and first half of the 19th centuries.

Between the date of the Religious census, when they were greatly worried by the decline in membership, and 1905 when they held a major conference in Leeds, the Quakers had relaxed some of their more stringent rules, in particular that of disownment for marrying a non-Quaker.

This stopped the overall decline, but there were some disquieting results when they compared morning attendance in 1851 with one 'first day' as Quakers referred to Sunday, in 1904. Membership within the York and Pickering Monthly Meetings had increased by about thirty percent. The Hull Monthly Meeting which covered the East Riding had dropped fifty percent. In the West Riding, there were mixed results, with no overall pattern obvious. A group in Lothersdale and another at Newhill had closed completely, Skipton was not referred to as closed, but had gone from twenty-four members to none. Ackworth, Dewsbury, Wooldale, High Flatts, Wakefield. Brighouse, Rawdon, Sheffield, Woodhouse, and Halifax had dropped significant numbers, some other places had lost just a few. Membership had increased considerably at Doncaster, Barnsley, Leeds, Addingham and Bentham, and by a few at other places. But even in the York area, where the highest number of people attended in 1904, the attendance was only four hundred and seventy-three.

84

The national conference held at the Meeting House in Woodhouse Lane, Leeds in 1905 to discuss 'The way forward' saw an audience of about a thousand people. There was a strong feeling in several sessions of 'hope and progress'. It was agreed, among other propositions, that the widening of Quaker beliefs and principals should be via the Adult School Movement, where they had already been extremely successful for many years in educating non Quakers. Previously this had provided a few new members, now it was felt with more concentrated effort on these schools and allied activities, they could be more successful at recruiting from their students.

30 Quakers in Leeds

The Quakers held pacifist beliefs, and continually worked for peace. Many had crises of conscience during both World Wars, but especially in 1914 - 1918. We are told that nationally, about a third of eligible Quaker men joined up. Many worked as ambulance drivers and did other kinds of war work. Some felt that they could not contribute in any way, and were imprisoned as conscientious objectors, receiving harsh treatment. Three such men belonged to the York Monthly Meeting.

During the 19th century the number of Catholics in England increased phenomenally. The abolition of all restrictive and punitive laws early in the century gave them the confidence to emerge from the religious shadows. They built new churches and schools, often helped by French émigré priests who had fled the French Revolution and its aftermath. This was when the Roman Catholic Public School, Ampleforth College was opened, to be followed some time later by nearby Gilling Castle preparatory boarding school.

In the early 19th century Irish men came into Yorkshire on a small scale, often to do seasonal work in agricultural areas such as the Wolds. When the potato famine struck in 1845, the few turned to many. A large number found work in the newly emerging town of Middlesbrough, but the greatest number made for the industrial areas of the West Riding. Even when the crisis in Ireland was over, people continued to come to England for a better life, though at a slower rate. By 1914, Roman Catholics were five percent of England's population, and they were mainly to be found in London, Lancashire, Tyneside and West Yorkshire.

The two types of Catholics, English and Irish took some time to integrate. In Yorkshire English Catholics had lived quietly in large towns, or in areas owned or previously owned by a wealthy, gentry Catholic family. Such places as Everingham and Holme on Spalding Moor in the East Riding, Egton and Ugthorpe, Gilling East, and South Kilvington in the North Riding, Spofforth, Aberford and Miton in the West Riding had all had a reasonably large Catholic community in the previous century. York had always been tolerant to its Catholic residents. Sheffield and Leeds too had sizeable English Catholic communities.

With the advent of a huge influx of Irish Catholics, the two Catholic Dioceses which had been established at Middlesbrough and Leeds had to find large numbers of priests. These were a mixture of English, Continental and Irish, all of whom had to adjust to their congregations. Two of these different types came together on Sunday Aug 13th 1911 when a young English Catholic who had just come down from Oxford with a first class degree, and was staying with a wealthy, protestant friend's family, went to mass. His diary records,

> 'Called at 7 o'clock, breakfasted by myself early, and caught a bus to Grassington station being the sole passenger. From there I got a train to Skipton, and reached the Catholic Church there about 10 o'clock. It is a stone church not particularly beautiful or ugly. At 10.30 there was sung Mass. Another priest, an old man preached the sermon. It was on the gospel of the day, the parable of the Pharisee and publican. It was simple and rather rambling and disconnected. After the offertory I was extremely annoyed by being asked whether I wanted change for a piece of silver I had put in the plate. Never have I heard of such a thing before.'

Catholics were still disliked by the dissenting churches. It took many years and encounters such as the following to dispel distrust. Mabel Gaines, who had been brought up in a staunch Methodist home, went by train to Egton Bridge, with her very new baby. She was going to stay with some relations at Wintergill, a farm on the moor top. They were supposed to meet her train. When she alighted there was no one there. Very worried, indeed frightened, she was taken to the home of some local people who were extremely kind to her. They sent word to Wintergill, and she was collected the next day. These people were Catholics, people she had been taught to fear and despise since she was a child. To ensure that such mistrust and bigotry was not passed on to her own family, the story was told and retold, and indeed did its work well.

In south Yorkshire, a Catholic church was built in the mining town of Denaby in 1895 to cater for the Irish miners employed there. The pastoral care was excellent. In the early 1900's, Yorkshireman Eddie Collins moved there with his parents. He remembers that almost as soon as they arrived the Catholic priest called on the family, 'because Collins was an Irish name.'

31 Scargill Chapel Skipton built in 1960

As the century progressed, some Irish prospered and moved out of the poor areas, into the suburbs. More churches were built to accommodate them, but these were never numerous, though often well filled on Sundays.

One of the most popular and growing evangelical groups of the time was the Salvation Army. Evangelical enthusiasm had always been warmly received by Yorkshire people, and with their positive attitude, message of hope and forgiveness, active social work, not to mention melodic hymns, (they were not above using the popular music of the times,) they were well established in most Yorkshire towns by 1900. Hull had seven places of worship for the Salvationists in the city, but they had some way to go to compare with the Methodists, who had of course been there much longer.

Also in Hull in the early 1900's were fringe sects, meeting in 'various temporary premises'. These groups called themselves the Plymouth Brethren, the Catholic Apostolics, the Christian Pioneers and the United Christian Bands.

In Leeds and Sheffield the Church of Jesus Christ of Latter Day Saints, more commonly called Mormons were found, along with the Exclusive Brethren and Christian Brethren.

32 Jehova's Witnesses take their message to the streets

George Gaines left England in 1912 to find work in Canada. He worked there for two years on the Canadian railroad. When he returned, a once devout Methodist had become a Jehovah's Witness. He contacted a local group in the Middlesbrough area. They had no church of their own at the time and they met at George's home from time to time. He remained a member of that church for the rest of his life.

These and other sects such as; the Christian Scientists, Mormons Spiritualists and Pentecostals originated in America. Some did well, others less so as the century progressed.

The only non-Christian churches in Yorkshire at the beginning of the 20th century were Jewish. Leeds and Bradford had the greatest numbers, since many were involved in the clothing industry. Hull also had a solid Jewish community. It had two synagogues, one for British Jews, the other used by foreign Jews. There were synagogues in Middlesbrough and Sheffield by 1900, but these had relatively small congregations.

33 Foxholes Methodist Church East Riding. The result of the decline in active church attendance which started after the First World War

The First World War, which started in 1914 and lasted for four years, brought change to many aspects of British life, not least in the area of religion. The people who returned to Yorkshire from the Continent had seen fighting in dreadful conditions and huge slaughter.

There had even been casualties at home. Scarborough was shelled by German ships on the morning of the 16th December 1914. This surprise attack killed seventeen people and injured over eighty. Though Yorkshire was out of reach of early aircraft, Zeppelin airships raided on sixteen occasions dropping bombs which killed in total one hundred and ten people in various parts of the county.

For many people who suffered during this period, their faith in God was a comfort. Spiritual and practical help was offered by most denominations, and gratefully accepted by people who were regular churchgoers, and by those who weren't. But for many, especially the ones who had lived through the hell of trench warfare, their religious faith was shattered. The poet Siegried Sassoon expressed it beautifully in his poem 'Prince of Wounds' which ends,

'Have we the strength to strive alone
Who can no longer worship Christ?
Is He a God of wood or stone,
While those who served him writhe and moan,
On warfare's alter sacrificed.'

Arthur Graeme West wrote in his diary in August 1916,

'I now find myself disbelieving utterly in Christianity as a religion, or even in Christ as an actual figure.'

Understanding this, and taking into account the loss of one in eight men who served in the British Armed Forces, it is not surprising that almost all churches saw reduced attendance after the Armistice. Figures for the Baptist churches in Yorkshire showed a moderate increase year on year until 1914. The membership declined by sixty-nine people between 1914 and 1918, and then the numbers continued to go down until 1927 when they show a further loss of about three per cent.

At Staxton, in the East Riding, the Primitive Methodists had held an annual camp meeting in June for many years. 'Musical accompaniment was provided by flutes, violins and a bass fiddle.' This continued through to the evening when people assembled near to the school and went in procession through the village singing hymns. The day ended with a faith supper in the granary at May Farm. This had always been looked forward to and well attended. There was never another such camp meeting after 1914.

Methodist Historian Rupert Davies believed that it was after the First World War that,

'Christianity lost its hold on the majority of the British nation.'

It would probably be more accurate to say that it lost its hold on the half of the nation who were actively Christian at that time.

The Spiritualist Church, which started in America in the mid-19th century was a belief in communication with the spirits of the dead, through a medium. It gained some support by the Edwardian period, and though fraud was occasionally proved, there were instances when no logical explanation was possible. Understandably it became very popular after the War, and the influenza epidemic which followed, when so many people were grief stricken from bereavement.

1920 saw an agricultural depression, followed by an economic slump the following year. People across the county in town and country were badly hit. Many churches struggling to survive themselves were at the forefront of the social work and charitable help that was so necessary. The recipients of help, sometimes began to attend a church or chapel for a variety of reasons, from gratitude to the hope of continuing to receive help.

Saint Paul's Mission in Scarborough as well as being a mission room was used for social functions and education classes. The cocoa house provided good food for those in need. It was clearly struggling in 1921, when the following appeared in Saint Mary's Parish Magazine,

'The Jumble Sale will be held at S. Paul's on Wednesday 4th May......*SEND ANYTHING!* If it will not sell we will be able to burn it, as we have no coal and the coke cellar is about empty.'

However for people who had work in the post war years, the standard of living rose. Competition appeared for the leisure time of people who had previously spent much of their free time in church activities. Cinemas and variety theatres abounded, cricket and football became popular both as participation and spectator sports, Yorkshire had a good cricket team, and a number of successful football teams to tempt young men away from church and chapel.

1931-1965

Against a background of economic depression and increasing unemployment, particularly in Yorkshire's industrial areas, Christianity of almost all denominations continued to decline. In rural areas, the Anglican Church had often had a strong hold, especially if the local landowner was opposed to non-conformity. In this period large estates were being broken up, and tenant farmers and their families, with a different landlord, no longer felt constrained to attend the Anglican Church.

At the same time labourers were often leaving their villages, looking for, better wages, or simply work. The work load of Anglican clergy in some places was reduced, but so were the clergy. Increasingly and for the rest of the century, in other areas many were having to look after two or more parishes. By 1931, there were five thousand less clergy than at the beginning of the century. Between 1931 and 1965 a further four and a half thousand were lost. This must reflect a decline in congregations, but may also reflect a lack of candidates for ordination.

After the Second World War numbers of children attending Sunday Schools fell. One alternative taken up by often younger Anglican clergymen (and other denominations), was to start a youth club. In both rural and urban areas, these places, which had activities such as table tennis, pop music and dancing, alongside the occasional film or slide show or talk, brought in the youth, not all of whom usually went to church. Some churches expected the young people to attend evening service once a month, some did not. All performed a very useful and occasionally spiritually rewarding service.

As was always the case, the personality of the vicar made a considerable difference. Judy Wilson a farmer's wife from near Scarborough was brought up in York. She said she was a Christian, but the family didn't go to church when she was a child in the 1950's because,

'The vicar was not a nice man.'

Unlike Non-Conformist organisations, where ministers worked a circuit, and moved every few years, Anglican clergymen could stay in the parish for the rest of their lives, and many did.

Methodism had had a slight boost to membership in the 1920's, indeed, the decline was not without its fluctuations for all the churches. An enthusiastic and charismatic minister or preacher could bring back the lapsed members and occasionally bring in the newly convinced.

For a number of years the three major Methodist churches had discussed amalgamating. The union happened in 1932 when they became the Methodist Church. This made them, by that one act, the largest denomination in Yorkshire.

There had never been any doctrinal differences between the Wesleyans, the Primitive Methodists and the United Methodist Church, and so in a period when they were certainly not expanding any longer, it certainly made economic sense.

The social status of the congregations varied slightly. Except in the inner city industrial areas, the Wesleyans were mostly middle class, 'respectable', professional, white collar workers. The United Methodists contained some middle class people but were mainly artisans and manual workers. The Primitive Methodists appealed to the miners and labourers in the industrial areas and the agricultural labourers. This did not present any special problem.

At the national level with a little adjustment to organisational matters, the union worked well. The different circuits, often within the same areas took some reorganisation. The main problem initially, was the chapels.

34 The Whitsuntide procession in Sheffield

Many congregations wanted to stay with their familiar buildings. The fact that the country was at war within seven years, may well have had something to do with it, but Sheila Roberts who attended the Greasbrough Primitive Methodist chapel in South Yorkshire in the 1950's, was never aware that there had been a union of the churches. There was a Wesleyan chapel in the same village, which soldiered on for a number of years with about four adult members and four children attending Sunday school.

In Scarborough it would appear to have been much the same, although it was the Primitive chapels which closed eventually, two in 1964 and two in 1967, and the Wesleyan chapels which survived. Clearly by the early 1960's, the continued drop in numbers, plus fewer of the older members, facilitated what had been started in 1932.

In the rural parts of the county where there was only one chapel, nothing much changed. Like the Anglicans, they lost membership because some younger people were moving into towns. Better wages pulled them in. Increased mechanisation; and properties, even in the thirties and forties, being used as second homes and holiday lets drove them out. Arnold Palliser who grew up in Swaledale wrote.

'My childhood memories of Gunnerside are still vivid and none more so than the Midsummer Summer Love Feast. Everyone wore their most colourful attire and fanciest hats, and all attended the afternoon and evening services in the chapel on the road down to the Swale.'

He goes on to recollect that all the exiles returned for this, and that the feast included tea and cheesecake. He tells us that, once the preacher was delayed, and an elder mounted the pulpit.

'Now then, sithee,' he said, 't'preacher's steps is lagging on't way ower fra Askrigg so us better have a sing song while he gets hissen here.'

He ended saying,

'The image of that crowded chapel, bathed in evening sunlight, and the sound of soaring voices has remained with me for 72 years.'

The high points of the urban areas were the Whitsuntide Sings, when all the chapels processed to a recreation ground. In Sheffield one destination for a Whitsunday Sing was Meersbrook Park, led by Meersbrook Band. Each Sunday school had its own banner and procession and either gave their members a breakfast before starting, or a tea later in the day. A service followed, The afternoon was always devoted to Sunday School Sports with each chapel having its own area for games and races.

In the village of Greasbrough as late as the 1950's, where there were two Methodist chapels and a very well supported Congregational Chapel, Parkgate Salvation Army Band led the children around the village, stopping at various suitable sites, such as the old mill yard, for a hymn and a prayer. Depending on the incumbent at the time, the Anglicans either joined in, or tried to sabotage the march using the Boys Brigade Band. Sadly these traditions had ceased by the early 1960's.

During the 1930's, there were still plenty of children attending Sunday School, but the parents were not necessarily church or chapel going themselves. The fathers looked on Sundays as a day of rest or leisure pursuits. One West Yorkshire Women's Institute member recalled,

'My mum went to the evening service at Church, and my sister and I went to Sunday School in the morning and afternoon.... And my father never went between marriage and death.'

One lady hated the 1930's when she and her mother lived with her maternal grandmother who was a strong Wesleyan.

'Sunday morning meant being dressed in my Sunday best clothes which were for Sundays only. At 10.30.a.m. we all had to go to chapel…. It was a cardinal sin to sit in the wrong pew, the ones nearest the preacher were reserved for the gentry, mill owners, shop owners, doctors, J.P.'s etc. So much for our so called democracy, even in the eyes of God you were segregated.'

Congregationalists and Baptists still saw respectable attendances, but though the decline was slow, it was relentless. Between 1931 and 1965 six Baptist chapels closed in Yorkshire, and those remaining lost forty-five percent of the 1930 membership.

The Quakers however reversed the trend for a time. Their efforts with the adult schools paid off. Hannah Clark of Doncaster remembered with pleasure an Adult School in 1954 where,

'It was a great sight to see the whole meeting house full of men and to hear them giving Sankey's hymns full blast.'

Year on year, membership increased until 1959 when the automatic membership of new children was abolished, which was reflected in the following year's statistics. But the numbers continued to drop from that high point and by 1965, had fallen by two thousand from the 1959 membership. Yorkshire membership declined slightly faster than the national membership, but it was not uniform, and new meeting houses were built at Keighley, Roundhay (Leeds), Wakefield, Bingley and Sheffield.

During this period Roman Catholics were a major Christian denomination in England. Though there were no longer great numbers of Irish immigrants coming into the country, there were always some. These now included women, many of whom were nurses.

At a time when Protestant families in England were limiting their families to one or two children, Catholics were forbidden to use birth control, and consequently often had large families. These factors made for a steady increase in Catholicism. Catholic churches were always full, Protestant churches increasingly less so.

By the thirties and forties there were sufficient Catholic schools to cater for their children. Only when middle class Catholics moved into the suburbs, where there was neither Catholic Church nor school, did their children attend state schools. As the century progressed this was dealt with, and Catholic churches were built on housing estates. At the same time, transport services improved, so all Catholic children were provided for.

The Jewish population, fairly large in Leeds and Bradford, much less so in other towns, increased slightly before war broke out in 1945. Because of persecution of continental Jews by the Nazis, thirty-three thousand came to Britain between 1933 and 1938. Hull again was a point of entry.

Barbara Rawson of York recalls the terror of even British Jews at the time.

> 'We had two Jewish ladies next door who used to swap fat, bacon and sweet coupons in return for tea, soap and margarine and washing powder. They were called Hannah and Sarah Cohen. In 1943, they were scared that Hitler was going to invade. One morning my dad noticed the curtains were still closed.....They found both sisters dead. They had killed themselves with gas. They were lovely folks, seamstresses by trade.'

'The Ecumenical Century' is how some church historians have referred to the 20th century. Alliances between the Christian churches had often started in the 19th century as a result of the overseas missionary movement. Progress in England was slow but the Edinburgh Missionary Conference on 1910 resulted in some committees which stimulated dialogue between the Anglican Church and the Free Churches, as the Non-Conformist churches preferred to be known by that time. Congregationalists and Presbyterians also engaged in talks about a possible merger, but at that time, they came to nothing.

Ecumenicalism, may have flourished in some places, but certainly not everywhere. A Women's Institute member remembered that in the 1940's,

> 'When I got older it was frowned upon to go out with a girl belonging to another denomination, i.e. a Baptist or Unitarian.....and even worse if the girl was Church of England.'

But some people happily attended more than one kind of church. Hannah Hauxwell of Baldersdale, and a celebrity in her later life, was brought up a Methodist. As a young woman she could appreciate the enthusiasm and energy of the preachers, reflecting that there were some outstandingly good ones, particularly before the war. She did not enjoy the 'tub thumping' types, and often wished they would shut up. She confessed she preferred Anglican services which were shorter.

A change in social attitudes, and the beginnings of secularisation could be seen early in the 1930's. It was estimated about five hundred thousand people were visiting the cinema on a Sunday and a test case proved this to be illegal, consequently a Bill was put through parliament to legalise Sunday cinema, with its promoters promising to do the same for theatres, lectures and exhibitions.

At about the same time Pope Pius XI called for Catholics to stem the tide of sexual liberation when he strongly condemned divorce and abortion, and attacked the cinema, reading novels, and the press. This may be just a hint that not all Catholics, who confessed their sins, were obeying the strictures laid on them by their religion.

Mass Observation, which recorded people's lives, attitudes and opinions between 1939 and 1945 gave a list of the nation's favourite activities in descending order of popularity. They were,

Staying in.
Reading.
Going to bed early.
Listening to the wireless.
Going to public houses.
Playing cards and other games.
Writing.
Smoking.

There was no mention of going to church.

Many Poles, Hungarians and Ukrainians even the odd German remained in England after the war. Some of these moved to Yorkshire to work in the textile industry and the coalmines. Per size of population, Bradford had the largest Polish community in Britain. These people were usually Catholics, and along with another influx of Irish, helped to continue to fill the Catholic churches in the late 1940's and 50's.

They were absorbed into the communities relatively easily, replacing the young Yorkshire men killed during the war. The following wave of immigrants who moved into the county in the late 1950's, and continued to do so for about twenty years, was a different matter.

Huge numbers of people from India and Pakistan, the West Indies and former British territories in Africa, arrived in the hope of making better lives for themselves and their families. Like the Irish before them, they moved to the industrial towns of the West Riding, with some going to Hull and Middlesbrough. They were prepared to do any work, and work long and unsocial hours, but nevertheless were not welcomed. What they also brought with them was a variety of beliefs and churches, some Christian, some not. It took them several years however before they could establish these.

Apart from fewer Methodist chapels due to amalgamation, the places of worship recorded in Kelley's Directory for Sheffield for 1965, do not reflect the falling in numbers of mainstream English Christianity, but do show how far what were considered 'fringe religions' at the turn of the century had come, and indeed endured and sometimes multiplied.

After the First World War, Spiritualism had become established as a church. Another dreadful conflict twenty-one years later, with the death and loss suffered, not just by combatants this time, possibly triggered further interest. Out of approximately two thousand, five hundred and fifty fatalities in Yorkshire between 1939 and 1945, seven hundred and sixty died in Sheffield. In 1965 there were seven spiritualist churches in that city.

Among other fringe churches which had gained ground, possibly at the expense of the better established churches were; the Church of Jesus Christ of Latter Day Saints, the Plymouth Brethren, the Elim church, two Pentecostal churches, The Four Square Gospel Alliance and the All Nations Tabernacle of the Church of God & Prophecy.

The Unitarians were well represented in Sheffield with three churches in 1965. Also interesting were the seven individual 'Wesleyan' churches, not included in the Methodist church's seven circuits around the city. They were an example of the churches which remained aloof and independent in 1932.

1966-2000

The last period of the 20th century saw the movement towards secularism accelerate. Where churches and chapels had somehow survived despite falling congregations and rising costs, it wasn't too obvious. From the 1970's church buildings became empty, and then if not in an area where they could be sold or used for some other purpose, become derelict.

Anglicans had the greatest problems, since their medieval churches were listed buildings and had to be maintained even if unused. 'Redundant Churches' was the term used for such buildings, usually found in rural areas. The 19th century churches were less of a problem, and by the end of the century many had been sold and converted into living accommodation or warehousing.

In spite of there being fewer churches, and despite the entrance of women into the ministry, first as deaconesses then as vicars, the numbers of parochial clergy were stretched. The result of this was one clergyman overseeing two or more parishes, or a group of clergy managing a much larger area, where the churchgoing parishioners were small in numbers.

35 Stape Methodist Chapel North Riding. Built c1876 now a private house

Instead of a minimum of two services every Sunday congregations were lucky to get one. Some parishes by the very end of the century would only see their vicar or curate once a fortnight. On other Sundays, services led by laymen and women appeared. Such expediencies do not bode well for the future. Since the Reformation, whenever protestant congregations have increased it has almost always been the result of an inspirational preacher or minister. When there is repeatedly no preacher at all, the outlook cannot be positive.

Non regular attenders still go to their parish churches for Christmas, Easter and the Harvest Festival. They will go to memorial services, and sometimes for services of celebration, and though on nothing like the same scale as in former years, for baptisms, marriages and burials.

Reliable statistics for this century are not easy to find, but in 2005 an English Church Census was taken which gave the number of churches and average attendances for Christian denominations, and though later than the period under scrutiny, and may as a consequence be less than they would have been in 2000, nevertheless show how the churches compared; and indeed, how small the congregations were. What the figures don't show is that such church and chapel goers were generally in the upper age range.

The attendances recorded at the Anglican churches in Yorkshire totalled seventy-one thousand, six hundred and sixty-eight, and were more than double those of the Methodists, who dominated protestant Christianity in Yorkshire at the beginning of the century.

Within Yorkshire, (although the Middlesbrough area was not included in the county figures), the North Riding, had the highest attendance with two point two per cent of its population. In the East Riding it was one point two per cent, and in the West Riding one point two per cent. The predominantly rural district of Ryedale, an area which encompasses, the market towns of Malton, Helmsley and Pickering, and the surrounding countryside, had the highest Anglican attendance at three point two per cent.

The Baptist church was the only formerly mainstream denomination which reversed the trend. From 1914 its membership had slowly declined until 1986, when they had sunk to seven thousand, two hundred and eighty-three. In 2005, those figures had almost doubled.

The largest congregations were found in Sheffield, Bradford, Leeds and the Kirklees Districts. These are the very areas which saw the largest number of immigrants to Yorkshire from the Caribbean and other former Commonwealth countries in Africa and Asia. It seems possible that if they had attended Baptist Churches in their countries of birth, they may well have gravitated towards them, once they were settled in England.

The Congregationalists, the Presbyterians and the Churches of Christ, after many years of discussion, joined forces in 1972. They formed the United Reformed Church. They too made multiculturalism a large part of their ministry. Their church of St. James in Sheffield, was one place which welcomed people from the West Indies in the 1960's, when this was by no means the case with other churches. Now all their churches make newcomers from outside Britain, welcome.

They have not enjoyed the same success as the Baptists. Their total attendance figures were five thousand, six hundred. These were the lowest figures by far of the denominations recorded. They had just over a third as many as the Pentecostal churches, who throughout the century, had been regarded as a fringe denomination, but who also may have benefited from Afro-Caribbean immigration.

Though a shadow of the force it once was, the Methodists were still a presence in some areas. The East Riding and the Harrogate district, (the Dales), had a reasonable number of regular attenders. Leeds, Bradford and Sheffield have maintained a strong presence, but they are not a high proportion of the very large populations of those cities. These had been the traditional strongholds of Methodism, and continue to be so, on a much reduced scale. Where once their chapels were numerous and obvious, to drive through Yorkshire today is to see those chapels used as supermarkets or carpet warehouses, or not to see them at all, demolition having been the chosen solution.

36 Greasbrough Methodist Chapel West Riding. It replaced a much larger chapel in the 1970's due to much smaller congregations

In 2005, the second largest Christian denomination in Yorkshire was the Catholics. Their figures had held up reasonably well, when protestant churches were seeing increasingly smaller congregations. From the 1980's onwards they too saw their numbers going down. The large families, which had helped sustain their denomination for years, were rarely seen, even among the most devoted Catholics.

Pope John Paul visited Britain in 1982, possibly to raise the Catholic profile and return to the faith some of the lapsed Catholics. He filled large venues, but preached mainly to the converted. He also met the Archbishop of Canterbury, and ecumenicalism was encouraged between the two faiths. This had local effects, as in East Ayton, where in the 1990's the Anglicans shared their church with local Catholics.

Twenty-eight years later, Pope Benedict also came to Britain. The Yorkshire Catholic Dioceses put out some statistics which showed that in the intervening years between the two visits, Middlesbrough Diocese had lost about two and a half thousand Catholics, twenty churches and nineteen schools. Catholic pupils, baptisms, marriages and reception into the church at age seven and over, were all down.

The Diocese of Hallam, in the West Riding had the same overall trends, except for school pupils, which had increased by just under four thousand. A healthy sign, but it is possible at least some of these children belonged to non-Catholic parents, who wanted their children to have a grammar school education.

At York, the Diocese of Clifton had an increased Catholic population of about eight thousand, and two more churches had been built. Even so the number of priests, schools, pupils, baptisms, marriages and reception into the church were all down, albeit not by a great deal. York had always favoured Catholicism, and at the end of the 20th century it continued to be an area where it survived better than other parts of Yorkshire.

As the former major denominations lost support, fringe denominations and sects survived, and even prospered. The Mormons, the Jehovah's Witnesses, The Spiritualists, and above all the various groups of Pentecostal churches, have a solid presence in most Yorkshire towns.

In addition there are new organisations, often non-denominational, but usually evangelical, giving spiritual succour on a small and local scale. Such is The Hollybush. A group of friends, who had received the 'Holy Spirit', were moved to buy Hollybush Farm near Thirsk in the North Riding. Their website tells us,

> 'We moved into the house in September 1968 and continued Friday night meetings. A prophetic word was given, "I will bring people from the north, south, east and west to be ministered to, and to minister." People began to come from all over the area who were hungry for more of the Lord, until we occupied the largest room in the house, (a bedroom) and spilled onto the landing and down the stairs. We then moved out of the house into the granary.'

Eventually they had premises to seat about two hundred and twenty people but that proved insufficient. The demand for much larger accommodation continued and in May 1992 a purpose built chapel was opened. People continue to attend services there. It is open to all. One couple were taken by a relative, a retired evangelical Anglican clergyman. They said when they went the congregation was about sixty. They enjoyed going and only stopped when they no longer had a car.

That there was still a need for evangelical preaching was seen in 1984, when Billy Graham the American evangelist visited Britain, using football stadiums as venues, and filling them. It was a highly organised event, 'almost slick' was a comment made by one lady who attended.

37 Sunbridge Road Mission in Leeds, an Independent Evangelical Church

Thousands went to hear him, and still more watched him on large screens, as did Hannah Hauxwell who had met him on the Terry Wogan show.

She enjoyed the organ music, was less keen on the pop music, which she thought was to 'pull in the youngsters'. Billy Graham, she said was 'most eloquent' and even on a screen, made such an impression on some people that they went up to the screen to dedicate themselves. Hannah, an elderly lady at the time, fell asleep.

That there are still many people searching for some meaning in their lives, was made obvious after the census was taken in 2011, when for the first time on a census, people had the opportunity to state exactly what if anything they believed in or practiced. There were nineteen organisations with a count of more than a thousand, outside the major religions.

The highest count went to 'Pagans', now generally believed to refer to a 'broad range of nature venerating religious traditions.' In Yorkshire there were over four and a half thousand, over three thousand being in the West Riding.

There were also well over a thousand 'Wicca' devotees, in the county. This became popular nationally from the mid-century being a modern form of paganism. 'These people meet in covens, to seek and practice magic' which is

38 Old Wife's Well Wheeldale Moor North Riding. A rag tree immediately adjacent to the ancient well which carries ribbons as tokens of petitions and wishes

39 The mosque and the minaret have become part of the Bradford skyline

aimed at doing good. In addition there are a number of people in Yorkshire who practice 'Witchcraft' and 'Druidism', similar sorts of organisation. Slightly worrying were the hundred and seventy 'Satanists' in the county.

By 1966 there were large communities of immigrants predominantly from the Indian sub-continent in Yorkshire. Some became established in Hull and Middlesbrough, but the greatest impact of this mass immigration was in the West Riding.

Bradford absorbed an estimated fifteen thousand people from Pakistan and four thousand Indians. A further estimated five and a half thousand each from the same places settled in Leeds and Huddersfield. Five thousand Pakistanis and two thousand six hundred Indians made their homes in the smaller towns of Halifax, Keighley, Dewsbury, Batley and others. By 1968 about another five thousand had settled in Sheffield. There were lesser numbers in Rotherham.

Quite quickly they found accommodation to use as Muslim and Hindu places of worship. As more Christian churches came up for sale, these were often bought, particularly by the Pakistani communities and converted for their use. By the end of the century they were building mosques to accommodate the growing Muslim population in Yorkshire, which had reached the figure of nearly three hundred and twenty-two thousand. A census which asked what religion the subject followed was taken in 2011. The Hindu figure for Yorkshire in the same year was just over twenty-three thousand.

Though very difficult in the early years, these areas have integrated to some extent, and avoided excessive aggravation between people of different religions. Community leaders and Christian churches work with Muslim leaders for the benefit of all, as they do with the Hindu, Buddhist, Sikh and Jewish communities.

The latter had had communities in Yorkshire since the late seventeenth century. They grew in the nineteenth century but were never large. By the end of the 20th century there were less than ten thousand, and these were overwhelmingly in Leeds and its surrounding area.

Secularisation, ecumenicalism and multiculturalism, three words which can virtually sum up what has most affected religion in Yorkshire in the 20th century.

In the middle of the 19th century about half the population did not attend church regularly, if at all. Though the population expanded to the end of the century and at a lesser rate beyond that time, there are indications that people gradually ceased to go to church regularly on a Sunday.

This did not happen at the same rate, and to all the churches at the same time. There were brief periods of recovery at various places at different times. A vicar, minister, pastor or priest could make an enormous difference, both in a positive and a negative way.

The rate of secularisation increased after the First World War and continued to speed up towards the end of the century, as more opportunities for leisure activities expanded. The garden centre and the shopping mall became the new church, the site of an accident or tragedy a modern shrine.

As the members, attenders and supporters of the various churches shrank, sheer economics, though this was no doubt not the only reason, indicated that it would be mutually beneficial if churches could amalgamate, or at least share premises. It became necessary that the different denominations should overcome their differences and focus on what they had in common.

Protestant churches led the way, rightly so since they had been the most divided. But as more was seen of this kind of cooperation, led from the highest levels, Catholics also began to talk to and eventually share services and social action with the rest of the Christian churches in Yorkshire

Parts of Yorkshire were barely touched by the large scale immigration of people who were not from a Christian tradition. The industrial parts of the West Riding along with Hull and Middlesbrough, were where non-Christian

40 A Goth wedding at Whitby.

places of worship eventually became part of the landscape. Initially empty premises including churches and chapels were used, but later some new mosques and temples were built.

Because people do not attend church regularly, it cannot be assumed they have no belief in God, Christian or otherwise. The century saw the growth of dozens of non-traditional sects, some of which became sufficiently numerous and well established to be called a denomination, some of which did not. Many of these were based on Christianity, some were not. Several of them have a strong international base while others are few in number, but these diverse associations emphasise that even in today's secular society many people have a need for a system of belief they can follow.

BIBLIOGRAPHY

W. Allott. The Leeds Quaker Meeting. Kendal, 1965.

C.J.F. Atkinson. Recollections from a Yorkshire Dale. London, 1934.

H. Chapman & P. Smith (eds). North Yorkshire Within Living Memory. Newbury, 1995.

B. Cockroft & H. Hauxwell. Daughter of the Dales. London, 1990.

F.L. Cross. The Oxford Dictionary of the Christian Church. London, 1957.

R.E. Davies. Methodism. Harmondsworth, 1963.

R.J. D.Harrison & G. Dixon. Guisborough before 1900. Guisborough, 1981.

S. Harrison. The History of Driffield. Pickering, 2002.

D. Hey. Yorkshire From AD 1000. London, 1986.

D. Hey. A History of Sheffield. Lancaster, 1978.

A. Howkins. Reshaping Rural England. A Social History 1850 -1925. London, 1991.

J. MacFarlane. 'Denaby Main: A South Yorkshire Mining Village' Studies in the Yorkshire Coal Industry. Eds. J Benson & R.G.Neville. Manchester, 1976.

L. Markham (ed.). Home Front Yorkshire 1939-1945. Barnsley, 2007.

J. Marsland. Over two Centuries of Methodism in Robin Hood's Bay 1747-1978. Lincoln, 1978.

D. Mercer. Chronicle of the 20th Century. London, 1989.

D. Neave. Port, Resort and Market Town A History of Bridlington. Hull, 2000.

N. Pevsner & D. Neave. Yorkshire: York and the East Riding. London, 1996.

C. Partridge (ed.). Encylopedia of New Religions. Oxford, 2004.

B. Pearson. A History of Conisborough and Denaby. Sheffield, 1997.

M. Rowlands. The Quakers of Kirbymoorside and District 1652-1990. Malton, 1990.

D. Rubenstein. 'York Friends and the Great War.'Borthwick Paper No. 96. York, 1999.

D. Rubenstein. Yorkshire Friends in Historical Perspective, An Introduction. York, 2005.

J. Rushton. The History of Ryedale. Pickering, 2003.

A. Russell. The Country Parish. Oxford, 1986.

J.F. Supple Green. The Catholic Revival in Yorkshire 1850-1900. Leeds, 1990.

T. Tastard. Anglo-Catholicism at the Beginning of the 20th Century. Gloucester, 2009.

C. Walker. A Glance Over My Shoulder. Barnsley, 1975.

INDEX